9 Innings of Hitting

Troy Silva

First published by Dog Ear Publishing
4010 W. 86th Street, Ste H
Indianapolis, IN 46268
www.dogearpublishing.net

ISBN: 978-1-4575-1957-4

This book is printed on acid-free paper.

Printed in the United States of America

"With *9 Innings of Hitting*, Troy has successfully integrated the several, yet distinct, components of the complex skill of hitting a well-pitched baseball. He covers the nuances of the biomechanics involved and ventures far beyond simply attributing hitting failures to mechanical flaws."

—Ed Cheff, retired baseball coach, Lewis-Clark State College

"It's about time someone lays out hitting with the entire truth. Troy's book has been needed in the baseball and softball world for a long time. Hands-down the best hitting book on the market today, *9 Innings of Hitting* is a must-read for coaches, players, and parents alike. It will stand the test for a very long time and be a valuable tool for beginners to pros."

—José Rijo-Berger, president of Rijo Athletics, former player with the New York Mets, and author of book, "Creating Winning Relationships Through Sports"

"A must-read for all coaches and players who want to understand how to develop a great approach to becoming a better hitter. I particularly love the chapters on the mental approach to hitting. Outstanding!"

—Ken Johnson, retired baseball coach, Walla Walla Community College and Washington State University

"When training with Troy in high school, he let me be me by allowing me to stay violent and aggressive as a hitter but under control. Now, working next to him everyday, my knowledge continues to increase as a hitting instructor."

—Marcus Faulkner, former high school All-American, 1st team All-NWAACC at Skagit Valley Community College, and current instructor at Rijo Athletics

"Troy helped me understand that while sound mechanics are important, they're only one piece of the puzzle that makes up a great hitter."

—Paul Gran, Miami Marlins

Photos

Thank you to the many players and their families who provided photos for this book. There is no better way to show the wide variety of athleticism, skill, personality, and commitment among my hitters. I'm so proud of all my players and thankful for the opportunity to help them improve their game.

Sam Lee

About Troy Silva

Troy Silva grew up in Atascadero, California. He played both baseball and basketball in high school and pursued baseball at Cuesta College, a small junior college in San Luis Obispo. Troy played baseball there for two years before being drafted by the Atlanta Braves in the 1994 amateur draft.

Instead of signing with the Braves, Troy enrolled at NAIA baseball powerhouse Lewis-Clark State College in Lewiston, Idaho. He played at L-C State for two years, including 1996 when he was a member of the NAIA national championship team and was named MVP of the NAIA regional tournament and NAIA World Series.

In 1997, the Cleveland Indians drafted Troy in the 18th round. He played professional baseball for six years before being forced to retire in 2002 after two arm surgeries.

After retirement, Troy joined his old college buddy, José Rijo-Berger, at Rijo Athletics, a baseball and softball training facility in Woodinville, Washington. He's been there ever since, teaching players of all ages about hitting and fielding, and coaches and parents about how to teach and motivate their players and children.

Troy is a devout Christian and thankful for the unbelievable gift that God has given him to be able to teach players, coaches, and parents as his everyday job. He can now see God's path and purpose for his life and why things happened the way they did. God didn't create Troy to be a big-league baseball player, but He did create him to be a big-league influence in people's lives, and Troy is extremely grateful for the opportunity.

Troy's goal in life is not to be a best-selling author but to honor God in all that he does. He tries to love others as more important than himself, which is definitely not easy to do. He prays that his actions are disciplined and that his flesh will never allow others to see an un-Christ-like example, giving them a reason to reject the love of God.

Troy's passion is to help people become better coaches, players, and parents. His hope is that this book will help people achieve whatever goals they have in hitting and life.

May God bless your endeavor!

Acknowledgements

Thank you to my Lord and Savior Jesus Christ for your grace and mercy in my life. I was the worst sinner, yet you chose to save me and then bless me with my beautiful wife, Denay. As if that weren't enough, you gave me three awesome kids, Trae, Ava, and J.J.

I have also been blessed in my everyday job at Rijo Athletics (which has never felt like a job, but a ministry). To my *mejor amigo,* José: I couldn't ask for a better boss, friend, or Christ-like example. To the Rijo staff: you are like family and I love you all. I am also very thankful to all of the Rijo families who have trusted me to teach their children about baseball and life over the years.

Thank you to Pastor Hutch and Antioch Bible Church for the realness and loving accountability. Thank you to all of my past coaches who influenced my learning process, and especially to Coach Ed Cheff for writing the foreword to this book.

Finally, thank you to everyone behind the scenes who helped make this book happen. I am truly a blessed man and deserve nothing, but for whatever reason God has graced me with amazing family and friends. Thank you!

The Silva Family

Contents

Foreword

By Ed Cheff

Shortly after the conclusion of the first baseball game ever played, theories began to develop as to the most expedient way for a hitter to "squarely hit a round ball with a round bat." Many years later, the search for the baseball hitter's "El Dorado" continues. And well it should!

It becomes the responsibility of every baseball player and baseball coach to seek out the skill-development path to a 33% success rate. In this book, Troy Silva successfully integrates many distinct components of the complex skill of hitting a well-pitched baseball.

While discussing the nuances of the biomechanics necessary to effectively control the entire strike zone, Troy ventures far beyond simply attributing hitting failures to mechanical flaws. He leads an excellent discussion of four key factors in a hitter's development at any level:

- An intellectual approach that recognizes a pitcher's arsenal of pitches and how that arsenal is deployed, and then combining that knowledge with pitch recognition and game-situational hitting as prescribed by the coach's offensive philosophy. Troy gives credence to the fact that a "hitting intellect" is a weapon that has a long reach and a sharp edge.
- Achieving rhythm and timing with the pitch delivery.
- Acquiring accurate information as to the speed and trajectory of the pitch.
- Demonstrating a learned level of emotional stability and mental toughness that correlates to a confident demeanor at the plate.

This last point is critical. Troy believes that fear of failure glows off of hitters who experience little simulated game pressure during hitting drills. He cites and supports the fact that coaches cannot talk players into demonstrating confidence. Confidence must be earned in a comprehensive teaching environment that demands focus and effort. Troy's plan for teaching and implementing how this fourth principle will be a hitter's greatest attribute is by itself worth the read of a great "baseball book."

Ed Cheff is the retired head baseball coach at Lewis-Clark State College in Lewiston, Idaho. In 34 seasons under Coach Cheff, L-C State posted a 1,705-430-2 record, the most wins by any college coach at one school. His teams reached the NAIA World Series 29 times and won 16 national championships, including in 1996, when Troy was World Series MVP. Coach Cheff was inducted into the College Baseball Hall of Fame in 2012.

Introduction

On Deck

If you've ever played baseball, you know the excitement that rushes through you when it's your turn to hit. From backyard Wiffle ball to Little League, high school, college, or even professional baseball, no matter where you played or what level you played at, there's just something about the feeling you get when the ball meets the barrel of the bat.

For me, it's somewhat addictive. It doesn't matter whether I'm hitting off a tee, hitting 105-mph fastballs from a ProBatter machine, or hitting softballs at an old-man slow-pitch game. I love hitting! And most people I know who have played baseball—kids included—love hitting just as much as I do.

In fact, I think the only people who have played the game and don't enjoy hitting are pitchers. And we all know why pitchers become pitchers in the first place, right? They can't hit, even though in their own minds they think they can. (I can talk about pitchers this way because I pitched in pro ball. And in my own mind, I can still hit!)

So why this infatuation with hitting? It's because hitting is the hardest athletic thing to do in all of sports. Yup, I said it, and will defend it with passion. Tell me another sport where you can fail seven out of 10 times and still be considered really good?

From Hope to Reality

As human beings, it's in our hearts to want to overcome obstacles. In the face of failure, we hope for success. Given how hard it is to hit a baseball, it's natural for ballplayers to want to master this ability. Hope keeps us working hard and swinging for the fences.

The reason for this book is to turn hope into reality for ballplayers by sharing my experiences. I've taught hitting to all ages, all skill levels, and to boys and girls. I've seen approaches that work and others that hurt players more than help them because they focus on swing mechanics rather than what each individual needs to succeed.

Whether you're a parent, coach, or player, we all want the athlete to maximize his God-given potential. Throughout this book I will show you the process and specific techniques that I use to make that happen. This same process is used by the staff at Rijo Athletics and has helped produce more than a thousand college baseball and fast-pitch softball players. We've coached more than 40 players who have been drafted by Major League teams in the last 10 years, and given more than 75,000 hitting lessons to players between 8 and 25 years old. I give you this brief history not to boast but to show you the scope of our success.

A Better Understanding

This book will also address the biggest questions regarding what is being taught in hitting today. Is the swing linear or rotational? Is there a difference between a baseball swing and a fast-pitch softball swing? Does watching a swing in slow motion really help? What can a hitter do to generate more power? How important is a hitter's mentality?

By answering these questions, I hope to equip you with a better understanding of how to maximize the athlete's potential and not just accept the myths and misconceptions being taught today. More importantly, I want to explain how to identify the real problems that affect a hitter's success. Often, these have nothing to do with swing mechanics.

The goal of this book is not to make you a professional hitting instructor but to give back the knowledge that's been given to me. I want to pass along the information you need to achieve whatever goals you have in this game we all love.

At the end of every chapter, I'll review what I covered in a short video—a visual aid to deepen your understanding. There also will be short videos on the terminology being used because I know the wording can get confusing at times if you aren't familiar with it. Hopefully, by seeing what I'm saying and describing the vocabulary more precisely, you can really grasp the information I'm talking about. Simply go to www.rijoathletics.com and click on the "9 Innings of Hitting" box—it will take you directly to the short video portion of the book or scan the QR code at the end of every chapter.

Enjoy your journey though this book. Remember, it's not about you or me, but about helping hitters achieve their desired goals.

Batter up!

Hitting is the hardest athletic thing to do in all of sports

Marcus Faulkner

Nico Rijo-Berger

Intro

Arrive On Time and On Plane

Understanding the hitter's main goal

What's the most important thing you need in order to be a great hitter? Think about it. Is it flawless swing mechanics? Amazing bat speed or vision? What about hand-eye coordination? The proper plan and approach? Mental toughness?

Those are all awesome answers, and none of them would be wrong because each of these attributes (combined with many others) is equally important to a great hitter. But they're only single elements in what is the most important aspect of all: the ability to arrive on time and on plane with the ideal bat angle.

I talk about this concept throughout the book, but let me give you a little introduction now about what it means to arrive on time and on plane.

The main goal for a hitter is to hit the ball hard on the barrel of the bat consistently. Arriving on time occurs when the hitter contacts the ball in the correct hitting area, which depends on the location of the pitch. "On plane" is best described as the bat contacting the ball on the same angle, or plane, of the pitch as it enters the hitting area. The ideal bat angle is created by the height, angle, and location of the pitch. The idea is to "square up" by keeping the hands above the barrel and letting the barrel angle level out behind the ball.

Arriving on time and on plane sounds easy enough to do, but doing it consistently is what makes hitting so hard.

Logan Moen

Depending on the pitcher, there can be six to eight feet of distance between possible release points from one side of the mound to the other, and another three to four feet of distance between the height of the release points. A left-handed pitcher who releases the ball from the left side of the rubber (which is two feet across) will create drastically different angles and movements on his pitches compared to a right-handed pitcher releasing the ball from the right side of the rubber. The same can be said about the height and arm angle of the pitcher. If the pitcher is tall and releases the ball from a higher arm slot, the pitch angles and movements will be extremely different compared to a shorter pitcher who releases the ball from a three-quarter or sidearm arm slot.

The hitter has a split-second to see the pitch and react to all the possible release points, angles, changes in velocity, movement of the ball, and the pitch location. That's why arriving on time and on plane is difficult, and why it must be the main focus of a hitter.

At the same, each element of the swing has to work with all the others in order for the hitter to make consistent contact. Think of arriving on time and on plane as the human body. The body doesn't function properly unless every part is doing its job. Some parts are more important than others, but even the smallest parts play a huge role. If something's out of whack—you roll an ankle or break a finger—your entire body just doesn't work right.

It's the same with hitting. Each element—mechanics, bat speed, hand-eye coordination, plan and approach, etc.—is important. They all have to come together in order to produce the desired outcome: arriving on time and on plane so the hitter can drive the ball with consistency.

Philosophies of Hitting: Linear vs. Rotational

Two main hitting philosophies circulate through the baseball and fast-pitch softball world today: linear and rotational hitting. I'm not going to tell you that either one is right or wrong—in fact, I've seen players helped tremendously by both approaches. But I will say that pushing these "styles" of hitting doesn't allow us to help each player individually.

My problem with linear and rotational hitting isn't necessarily with *what* is being taught but *how* it's being taught. A coach will read a book or take an online hitting course and become infatuated with one particular hitting style. He'll then take that style and try to apply it to every player regardless of age or ability.

That's issue No. 1: not all hitters are the same. Just go and watch a big-league game. Each hitter uses whatever "style" works for him individually. This leads to my next problem with hitting philosophies, which is how coaches relay information to hitters.

I'm sure if you talked directly to the people who came up these hitting philosophies they could articulate them precisely and clearly. But most people don't know how to teach hitting let alone one particular principle or approach. They may be able to describe or mimic what a swing should look like but have no idea how to help the hitter develop the specific elements of the swing necessary to produce the desired outcome.

When you're teaching someone how to hit, you have to start by understanding who you're teaching. A high-school hitter may know what you mean when you tell him to swing the bat on the same plane of the pitch and slightly uphill (a rotational approach). But relay that information to a Little Leaguer and he'll hear, "Drop your hands, swing up, and try to hit a bomb." You're only going to create more problems.

Another example would be telling a hitter to not really "rotate" his hips because it will cause him to pull off the ball (a linear approach). If that hitter is 6-foot-3 and 230 pounds (like the big-league hitters you see in pictures), he can probably get away with not fully rotating his hips. But telling a 14-year-old kid who's 100 pounds soaking wet not to use every ounce of power in his legs just for the sake of sticking to a philosophy, or because some big-leaguer twice his size does it that way, is absurd.

I can go on with examples about why I disagree with teaching one style of hitting to all ages and abilities. I guess if hitting were all about looking pretty I'd lean toward the linear philosophy because most linear hitters I see look like their swing belongs in a magazine. If you're mostly concerned with how you look, you probably won't generate bat speed or power, and you won't have the mentality to deal with certain pitches and pitch locations. On the other hand, I'd choose the rotational style if I was facing batting-practice fastballs in a home run derby because I could get away with some of the problems rotational hitting brings. My biggest problem is that the way the swing is being explained isn't compatible with what the hitter should be thinking about.

Just Call It 'Hitting'

In my experience, the actual mechanics of the swing should be rotational and linear. In fact, depending on the individual hitter, the swing should combine elements of both. For example, hitting an inside pitch requires a rotational movement while hitting an outside pitch requires a linear movement. A hitter may combine these two philosophies in one swing, explosively "rotating" the hips to create quickness to the ball, while taking a "linear" hand path to the ball to keep the bat on the same plane of the ball longer.

Call it "rotanear" hitting. Or "linational." To me, it's just hitting.

This brings me to my biggest complaint about the way hitting is taught in baseball and fast-pitch softball: "hitting" isn't being taught at all! Coaches focus on teaching a method rather than identifying a player's strengths and weaknesses and conveying what he needs to be successful.

The Real Key to Hitting

The funny part about all this talk about philosophies is that actual swing mechanics play only a small role in a hitter's success. People will defend their style of hitting like the world depends on it, but most don't understand what it takes to become a true hitter. Pretty swings are easy to develop—just give me an hour—but looking better doesn't create desirable results on the field.

Developing quality hitters begins with a commitment to creating a consistent swing. A swing is easier to duplicate when the mechanics are personalized to each hitter's needs. The process can take a long time, but these mechanics must be mastered in order for the player to advance into the more important aspects of hitting.

This next part of the chapter will give you a better understanding of what various elements of the swing do.

Remember, mechanics will differ from player to player. This information is by no means the only way to do it, but it is a proven, widely accepted view on the basics of hitting mechanics. So let's dig in to the techniques used by myself as well as the staff at Rijo Athletics that have produced thousands of successful hitters.

Mechanics Explained

A hitter's swing has many moving parts. Some are necessary, like loading, body-weight shift, backside staying bent, hands above the barrel, head behind the ball at contact, and extension through the ball, to name a few. Some don't have to happen and depend purely on the personal preferences, comfort, strengths, and weaknesses of the individual, like striding or no striding, top hand on or off through the finish, wider or shorter base with the feet, etc.

It's important to focus on the mechanics that most affect the hitter's ability to arrive on time and on plane. I'll get into detail to help you understand what each of the main elements of a swing actually do and what we really should be teaching. As a coach, here's what I look for:

Setup and Stance

I've just about seen it all. Open stances, closed stances, wider feet, feet closer together, hands high, hands low, a lot of bat movement, no bat movement, stiff statues, wet noodles, the list goes on and on! Sometimes that's just one kid! In one week!

I can't say that one particular setup and stance will deliver more success but I will tell you that setup and stance can play a major role in why certain success is not achieved.

When teaching setup and stance, you have to keep in mind the hitter's age, skill, and what feels comfortable. If the hitter isn't comfortable, he won't feel confident! Hitters also like to emulate their favorite players, so don't be too critical or force them to set up a certain way. Remember, what works for you might not work for someone else.

That doesn't mean coaches should let hitters do whatever they want, either. With the setup and stance, I definitely err on the side of making some things mandatory to start. Establish good technique and then, as hitters advance, they can create their own little "swagger." As long as the swagger doesn't affect their swing mechanics, it will probably stick with them throughout their playing career.

As a coach, work on the setup and stance from the ground up. If the foundation (legs and feet) is unbalanced and inconsistent, the hitter's hand-eye coordination will be inconsistent as well. Let's break down the lower and upper body:

Lower body: Start by checking plate coverage and their position in the batter's box. There's no exact science on where to stand in the batter's box, but you want the hitter to be able to hit the

Jason Todd

ball consistently whether the pitch is inside or outside. You want the hitter to set up based on his own personal strengths. For example, a hitter who hits inside pitches better should stand a little bit closer to the plate to make the outside pitch easier to reach and vice versa.

The feet should start shoulder-width apart or wider, and lined up straight. The stance should be straight toward the pitcher or open, but not closed (this isn't the 1980's—not too many hitters hit closed off anymore) so they can still get to a fastball inside consistently. The knees should be bent depending again on comfort, and the weight should be centered or slightly on the backside. The consistent setup of the lower half (legs and feet) of the body allows the hitter to maximize his power and balance throughout the swing.

Upper body: The hands should start where the hitter feels most comfortable, knuckles included, as long as the top hand is not "choked" on the bat. The hand placement is usually around shoulder high and back more toward the back shoulder. The shoulders should be as straight as possible toward the pitcher, but a little open or closed probably won't hurt.

The back elbow should be behind the hands, relaxed, and no higher than the back shoulder. The elbow being shoulder high or a little lower is most common. The bat angle needs to stay in that 45-degree range, not straight up and down or parallel to the ground (somewhere around ear-high). The hitter's vision is one of the

Garrett Patterson

most important factors to all of hitting, so make sure that the head is straight, still, and in such a position where he can see the ball with both eyes.

If players can take these basic rules for setup and stance and then add in their own "swagger" they'll have the foundation they need duplicate their swing consistently and achieve success.

The Load

What is the purpose of a load? A load is the action of the player getting ready to hit. There are two main reasons why a hitter must load. The first reason is for timing. The second is that loading helps generate more bat speed and power.

To say that there is only one way to load would be like saying there is only one way to hit, and I've already covered that fallacy. I've worked with hitters who load a little, load big, load with more hands, load with more legs, load hands-up, and drop hands down. I may not agree with some of these loading techniques, but the reality of "hitting" is reflected in the different ways hitters get themselves ready to hit. As a coach, it's important to recognize whether the hitter's technique interferes with his ability to arrive on time and on plane. The way the hitter loads may cause him to be consistently late on a good fastball, out in front on pitches (rolling over), popping up, or swinging at bad pitches. On the contrary, I've coached hitters who can mash despite not loading in a "traditional" way. They succeed because they load the same way every time and then let their natural abilities take over.

No matter what loading technique a hitter uses, the point is that the load is an important piece to a great swing. I encourage all levels to start with this basic approach:

The chest should stay "stacked" (or upright). The focus is to not load in toward the plate, which will help, again, in the hitter's ability to control both sides of the plate. The hitter should load back, but how far back is a matter of the hitter's preference and comfort. Typically, the overall load is in the 1- to 6-inch range. Again, it's not about a precise measurement, it's about getting ready to hit.

I prefer more of a load in the legs, with a little movement in the hands, making sure the hitter goes straight back rather than "twisting" or "wrapping" back behind the body. When the hands load, there should be a slight angle with the barrel head of the bat somewhere close to above the head. The load should be balanced, the eyes not bouncing up and down, and the back elbow should be up (somewhere around shoulder-high). Since one of the main reasons for loading is to create a timing mechanism readying the player to hit, it is always better to load early rather than late.

By keeping to these main principles, and finding a way that works individually for the hitter, you will find that a consistent load will be highly beneficial to helping the actual swing itself.

Shift and Stride

One of the most overlooked elements in hitting mechanics is the body weight shifting back to center.

I've said this probably a million times: "a little bit back, to where you started." What this means is that however far back the hitter loads, there must be a weight shift to get back to where he started.

Too many coaches or hitting instructors see the hitter getting too far out in front and so they work on "staying back." The problem is, they load back and "stay back." I myself am guilty of telling hitters to "stay back," but understand that the "stay back" part of the swing happens after the body weight shifts back to where it started. If you analyze the swing of a big-league hitter, you'll see that no matter how big or small the load is, his weight always shifts back to where it started.

If we taught the hitter to load, shift his weight, and then stay back, there probably wouldn't be as many out-in-front swings because the hitter would stay through the ball longer. We must be able to relay this information properly because if the hitter doesn't shift, the swing will become more circular, and I think everyone can agree that the swing should not be circular.

What about the stride? How does the body shift at all if the player chooses not to stride?

Whether a hitter strides or not is one of those mechanical things that are determined by the preference of the hitter. If the player chooses not to stride, it's usually based on comfort, or because it helps to fix a certain problem. I call it a "no-stride" or a knee roll. Both ways start with the feet wide already. The hitter will either just lift up and then drop the front foot to the ground, or keep the front toe on the ground when the load occurs and then quickly drop the front heel to the ground when the swing starts. Either way, if the hitter chooses not to stride, the load and shift still must happen for power and timing. The load and shift are usually smaller because of the no-stride.

If the player likes to stride, there are only a couple of things to remember. If the stride gets too big, the hitter can lose a tremendous amount of power through the legs. He should also stride straight toward the pitcher. If the stride steps out away from the plate or dives in toward the plate, the player may have trouble hitting certain pitches (inside, outside, etc.). If the hitter likes a "leg kick," that too is OK unless it creates timing issues. In fact, I see numerous hitters who are very successful and have a big leg kick. Unless it creates timing issues, the size of the stride or leg kick shouldn't be a big deal when teaching the mechanics of the swing. I would only make changes if there were a problem with a certain aspect of the swing.

Hips and Hands

This is where the mechanics of the swing get interesting.

My only job for the past decade or so has been giving baseball and fast-pitch softball lessons at Rijo Athletics. Hitting is my focus but I also teach infielding and have taught pitching, weight training, and speed and agility. Over the years, no topic has stirred more debate than the mechanics of the hips and hands. I've heard some crazy ways that people teach this subject, and some of them are rather humorous. One former player told me about the "buckle your seatbelt" swing. Yup, the coach actually told the player to swing like you are putting on your seatbelt. When I heard this, I almost dropped to the ground because I was laughing so hard! If you can just picture what that would look like, and then see the player trying to swing like that, you would almost die laughing, too! I've heard many other outrageous descriptions, but that one takes the cake.

But really, why does this topic create such a big stir? Besides the fact that I think people just like to argue, there are good questions about the hips, hands, and hitting. Which one starts the swing, the hips or the hands? Do the hips rotate or not? Should the hands chop down, or drop and swing uphill? There are many more. I answer these questions all the time during clinics and I address them in Chapter 6 on slow-motion video. For now, I'll give you an idea of what needs to be taught regarding the hips and hands.

Let's start with the hips. Yes, it is true that the hips start the swing. However, the way we teach it to the hitter is extremely important. The hitter needs to focus on the hips and hands working together (at the same time). Concentrating on one without the other will cause the swing to get long.

The hips do actually "rotate" to the ball depending on location of the pitch. What that means is that the hips should rotate fully on an inside pitch and only about 3/4 of the way on an outside pitch. In either location of the pitch, the hips stay "squared up" to the ball.

A common fallacy in hitting is that the hip rotation causes the back foot to "squish the bug" (or in other terms, the hips and feet rotate in a circle). In reality, the hips don't do this. The "squish the bug" terminology, which I personally have used, is more geared toward really young hitters who have no idea what the backside really is. If the hips actually did rotate in a circle, then the hands would be long to the ball with no extension.

Hip rotation is an explosive movement, driving the backside hip forward and the backside knee downhill toward the front toe. The hitter shifts that power forward, hitting against the front leg. Once the hitter can duplicate this action over and over, the next step in the process is to learn how to speed up the hips. "Quick hips" is what generates explosive bat speed and allows the hitter to see the ball a little bit longer for better pitch recognition. By being consistent in keeping the backside bent, the lower half of the body can stay balanced, explosive, and allow the hands to accurately do their part in the swing.

Now let's talk about the hands.

The hand path to the ball has mainly been described in two very different, almost opposing ways. One is a chopping, downward motion to the ball, which supposedly creates more backspin. The other is to try to get the bat head on the same plane as the ball, creating more of an "uppercut" in the swing. Which one is right? Again, I say neither. I think the difference comes down to the way people try to explain the two.

The "chopping" path to the ball is taught to hitters this way: The quickest way between two points is a straight line, and I agree. In this case, the straight line is not down, it's forward. So the hands don't chop down at the ball, they drive forward! As far as the "backspin" is concerned, the hitter can create a lot of backspin by chopping. However, this type of backspin will have no force behind it because the barrel of the bat goes down through the ball instead of getting behind it. Real backspin is created by the barrel head staying on the same plane as the ball as long as possible through the extension of the swing.

On the opposite end of the spectrum is this "uppercut" path to the ball. It's true that the swing should have a slight upward movement through the hitting zone (and I mean slight). This is necessary to get the barrel head on plane since the ball is usually coming out of the pitcher's hand on a downward path. However, with

Kenley Ackerman

my experience in teaching hitting, players who try to swing like this are almost always too long and slow to the ball because their hands never really attack the ball out front.

To sum up what the hands should do during the swing is simple: don't chop to the ball and don't upper-cut to the ball. Instead, attack the hands forward and let your barrel head level out behind the ball.

Extension and Finish

Extension happens during the part of the swing where the bat contacts the ball. At contact, the player's arms "extend" out toward the pitcher and the top hand whips the bat through the ball, keeping the bat on the same plane of the ball as long as possible. A good visual is to pretend the ball has a tail on it, and the tail is made of four more baseballs. The goal should be to drive the barrel head through not just one ball, but all five. This action of hitting through all of the balls is extension.

Extension is important because it keeps the hands squared-up to the ball longer and generates force from behind the ball, which helps create the proper backspin. Most of all, extension allows the barrel head of the bat to stay longer in the hitting zone. This gives the hitter more room for error in the timing of the contact. An example of this is when the hitter mishits the ball on the top or bottom half. If there is extension, the ball will still be hit hard, just not on a line.

Another benefit of extension happens when the hitter is fooled by the pitch, or gets out front, usually on some type of off-speed pitch. The normal contact point (depending on location of the pitch) should be some-

Grayson Livingston

where close to where the stride foot plants. If the hitter gets fooled and contacts the ball too far out front, extension will keep the bat on the same plane as the ball longer, still allowing successful, solid contact.

During this extension process the head should stay down as long as possible until the back shoulder naturally brings it slightly back up. I think one of the hardest things to do in all of hitting is to attack the ball with the backside of the swing and still be able to track the ball with your eyes all the way into the hitting zone without your head pulling off. This is why the swing must finish high. Finishing with the hands up and over the front shoulder enables the head to stay down and the eyes to see the ball longer. Extension through the ball and a high finish go hand in hand.

It's up to the hitter to decide whether the top hand should come off or stay on the bat after extension. There is no right or wrong in this area, and a lot of good hitters can do both. I prefer hitters to work first on keeping the top hand on through the swing because it forces them to learn how to let the ball travel, and it speeds up the swing. If a good hitter is fooled on a pitch, most of the time the top hand will naturally come off through the finish anyway. Let the hitter decide what feels best and only change it if it is causing another problem.

Bottom of the 1st

The focus of this chapter is to explain the mechanics of the swing, clear up some misconceptions, and give you practical ideas you can work on yourself.

Proper swing mechanics are vital to the development of good hitters. However, just because a hitter has good swing mechanics doesn't automatically mean he can hit! It can take a long time to come to a point where a hitter's swing mechanics are consistently repeatable. It can also take a long time to iron out mechanical flaws.

Remember, not everyone is the same, and some specific mechanics will vary. As coaches, we should make sure each hitter feels comfortable and enable him to hit to his individual strengths and athleticism. Try hard not to clone hitters into one specific "style" of hitting, but instead allow each hitter to create his own little swagger. Repeating swing mechanics consistently is the first step in helping hitters accomplish their goal of arriving on time and on plane.

—*End of the 1st*

Just because the hitter has good swing mechanics doesn't mean he can hit!

Chapter 1

2nd Inning

What the Hitter Really Needs

Why swing flaws happen and what coaches can do about them

(Please note that the pictures in this chapter represent the correct way the swing should look,
NOT the swing flaws that are being talked about.)

Understanding the functional movements of the swing takes an unbelievable amount of time. Learning how to convey that information properly can take even longer.

After playing college baseball for four years and then professionally for another six, I was sure that I could teach others how to hit. Early on, when I first started instructing, I tried to make everyone hit the way I liked to hit. I had this idea that swing mechanics were the most important things to teach a hitter, and that hitters would succeed if they could just copy the mechanics I was teaching them. It was like I was running a factory making robots specifically designed to perform the most popular swing mechanics of that era.

With time, I came to realize that most of the hitters I worked with were not really getting better, just looking better. I was doing players a disservice by focusing on technique and not what each individual actually needed. Today, after teaching hitting as my everyday job since 2003 (that's more than 25,000 lessons), I'm constantly seeking new and better ways to help hitters. It starts with the understanding that all athletes are different, and in teaching hitting, we have to be able to adapt to who we are working with.

Being able to explain the same ideas in different ways is crucial when you work with players of different ages and skill levels. How something is explained or taught to a 10-year-old player probably should not be the same as working with a college or pro athlete. The individual hitter's abilities play a huge role in what should and shouldn't be taught.

I'm not saying that we need to teach a different philosophy to different skill levels. In fact, I teach the same overall functions whether the hitter is a Little Leaguer or a pro. I am saying that we need be careful with how and what we teach to different levels of hitters.

For example, let's look at a 10 year old and a 19 year old, both with great swings and a tendency to pop the ball up. A coach who is consumed with mechanics may look at that result and conclude that both hitters are "dipping" (I'll explain this swing flaw later in this chapter) and start tinkering with their swings. But what if the 10 year old is popping up not because he is dipping but because five games ago he hit his first home run ever and now is trying to clear the fence all the time? What he really needs is a change in mentality, not his swing. The 19 year old simply may need to lay off the high pitches, which are causing him to pop up. There may be nothing wrong with his mechanics, but his pitch selection and pitch recognition need work.

This shows the importance of identifying the real problems affecting each individual hitter, and that the flaw is not always mechanical. The focus of this chapter is to help coaches identify a hitter's personal weaknesses and to explain why these weaknesses may occur. This is probably the most important chapter for understanding how to really instruct hitting on a more advanced level.

How to Recognize Swing Flaws

Most coaches and even parents know a poor swing when they see it. I'm always hearing from coaches about specific players and their mechanics. Parents also give me their opinion of what their child is doing

Trever Morrison

wrong. And you know what? Sometimes they're right! What most coaches and parents don't understand, though, is why these mechanical flaws happen. Once we know that answer, we'll be on our way to giving the hitter what he really needs.

The first step is to watch the hitter swing at a game-like pitch. I don't mean he has to be playing in a game, but some type of live pitch is necessary. It's tough to analyze a hitter when he's only hitting off a tee or doing soft toss. I see thousands of swings daily, and what I see hitters doing in the cage does not always translate into what they're doing on the field (this is especially true with high-school varsity, college, and more advanced hitters). This is exactly why we need to watch the hitter's game at-bats.

Recognizing why swing flaws occur is hard, but until we do the hitter will struggle with the same problems again and again and won't understand why consistent success never comes. Once we've identified flaws and determined what's causing them, the hitter can work on specific things in order to find consistency at the plate.

The most common mechanical problems are: pulling the head and hands off the ball; getting long to the ball, or casting; rolling over, or not getting extension through the ball; lunging; dipping; and wrapping. The common non-mechanical issues that cause these swing flaws include timing, being scared of the ball, pitch selection, and pitch recognition. Most of these flaws are connected directly to other bad habits, causing a "circle effect" that I explain later in the chapter.

It's important to understand what these problems look like and why they may be happening so you can properly relay correct information to the hitter.

Pulling the Head Out

Go to any baseball or softball game, sit in the crowd for an inning, and I bet you'll hear a parent, coach, or even players in the dugout scream at a hitter to "keep your head down!" or "keep your eye on the ball!" I even hear this in Spanish when I go to Nicaragua for our company mission trip every year! If pulling the head out is so easy to recognize then why do so many hitters have such a hard time with it? Keeping the head down all the way through contact is hard to do because the rest of the body is aggressively rotating forward in the opposite direction of the head.

The most common reason the head flies out is a long swing (a great example of how one mechanical problem can lead to another one). This is why technique is so important. The swing requires parts of the body to work together to form one fluid function. If one of those parts is messed up, it can cause others to mess up as well. For example, if the hitter has a long swing, he has to find a way to get the barrel to the ball so he won't get jammed. Stepping the stride foot out and pulling the head out are not ideal in terms of technique, but in this case are necessary for the hitter to make square contact. So, by having a long swing, the hitter is forced to pull his head out in order to hit the ball hard. What we see is the hitter "not keeping his head down" during the swing, but how to fix it is by working on not "casting" the hands to the ball.

Another reason the head pulls out is because of the hitter's mindset. What I mean is that some players cannot walk to the plate without looking at the outfield fence and deciding to go for it. In all reality, the long ball is what a lot of hitters strive for even when they know they probably can't hit it that far. I work with hitters all the time where the home run is detrimental to their success. They hit one out and from that point on think they're Barry Bonds. The trouble is, they become more like Mary Bonds!

Swinging for the fences only creates bad habits, the worst being pulling the head off the ball. I definitely can relate: from tee ball until my Junior year in college (about 16 years), I tried to hit a home run in almost every at-bat. I can only imagine how much better I could have been if I had a different mindset.

There are other reasons why the head might pull out during the swing. It may be as simple as bad pitch recognition, or the hitter trying to pull the ball. Whatever the case, there's more to it than what the common fan might see. Next time you see a hitter not "keeping his eye on the ball," know that he's not doing it on purpose. Something deeper is causing it to happen.

Casting

For most coaches, the "casting" motion is easy to recognize. The best way to describe it is to think of the swing path as a circle, with the first movement of the hands going out or casting away from the body. Another way to explain it is "getting long to the ball." A "long" swing seldom allows the hitter to hit the ball square, and as a result he gets jammed (hits the ball on the handle instead of the barrel), rolls over ground balls to his "pull" side (third base for righties, first base for lefties), or hits balls too late (foul or to the opposite field).

In my experience, there are four common reasons why hitters cast their hands and get long to the ball during a swing. The first is that the hitter is stiff and has a tendency to lock up his shoulders. For an idea of what this looks like, shrug your shoulders and hold them there. Then, swing the bat by rotating only with your abs. Your hands will always swing to the ball in a circular motion, creating a long swing.

The next reason is when the front arm locks out right before the hitter starts to swing, usually during the load. I see this with hitters who play golf. Take your front arm and put it back to where you would start your swing. Now lock it straight out and act like you are taking a swing at the ball. Your hands, again, have to "cast" out away from your body before going forward.

A third reason is that the hitter twists during his load. When the hitter gets his hands too far back behind his body, that twisting movement in his upper body will also force his hands out and around his body in order to contact the ball.

Finally, there's timing. Timing affects casting when the hitter loads too late. He creates a longer path to the ball when he has the momentum of the load going back and then tries to swing the bat forward. To put it in simple terms, don't let the hitter load and swing at the same time. If the timing of the swing is late, it will sometimes result in a long swing to the ball.

Other things can cause "casting" in the swing: the head pulling out, "lunging," seeing the ball too late, hitting the ball too deep, slow bat speed, striding out, being scared of the ball, bat too heavy or long, bad bat angle, and the list goes on. However, the things I covered are the most common for more advanced hitters. Again, the focus here is to not just recognize the swing being long to the ball, but to find out why.

Rolling Over

"Rolling over" occurs when the hitter's top hand "rolls over" the bottom hand at contact, creating a lack of extension through the ball. This is the explanation that coaches give most frequently after a ground ball—the hitter "rolled over" on his swing. Believe it or not, it *is* possible to hit the ball on the ground without rolling over. The hitter can take a great swing, with good extension, and simply miss-hit the ball. Just because the ball was hit on the ground does not automatically mean the hitter "rolled over."

The most obvious indication that a player is rolling over is when he consistently finishes the swing lower than his front shoulder. If the swing finishes low, the hitter is not getting extension. This is why extension is so important. Extension through the ball forces the hands to finish higher, not allowing the top hand to roll over at contact.

The three most common reasons why "roll overs" occur are casting, lunging, and hitting the ball too far out front (which goes with the mindset of always trying to pull the ball).

With casting, when the hitter gets long *to* the ball he will always be shorter *through* the ball. "Short to it, long through it," is what I say to describe the action of the hitter's hands getting to the ball quickly, and staying long through the ball (extension). However, if the casting motion to the ball occurs, more than likely the hands will "roll over" at contact. I've never seen a hitter who can "cast" his hands and still get good extension through the ball.

Lunging happens when the hitter's front knee bends and the body weight gets too far out over the front foot (I cover this in depth later in the chapter). When the body weight lunges too far out, the hitter's hands usually drag behind the body. The bat contacts the ball too deep, causing the hands to roll over. Lunging also may cause the hitter to hit the ball too far out in front.

This leads to the third reason why rolling over may occur. When the hitter's contact point gets too far out in front, the arms can extend only so far before the top hand must "roll over" and finish the swing. There are various reasons for this, but the hitter's desire to pull the ball is the most common. When the hitter has a pull mentality, his approach creates swing mechanics that pull the head, hips, and hands off the ball. As a result, he tends to roll over.

Once we know why the hitter is rolling over, the place to start to fix it is in the finish. Coaching the hitter to finish the swing higher (over the shoulder) forces the hands to get better extension, and when there is extension through the contact point, there are less "roll overs."

Not all roll overs are bad. Personally, I'd rather have someone roll over than pop up. Pop-ups are always outs, where ground balls are a better opportunity for the player to get on base. I don't know one coach who

Carson Ryder

would be upset with a player who crushes a hard ground ball through the 6-hole and gets a hit out of it. And in situational hitting, a rolled-over ground ball can produce a run. The focus, though, is to create extension through the swing that will allow for more consistent, squared-up contact.

The reality is that all hitters will roll over. Pitchers will make good pitches and hitters will get out in front. But, if there is extension through the swing, these roll overs will be less likely to happen, giving the hitter more opportunity for success.

Lunging

Hitters want to hit the ball hard. To do this, momentum plays a key role because some sort of shift in body weight is mandatory for timing and bat speed. But don't confuse shift with lunging.

Lunging happens when the body weight shifts and doesn't stop. Instead of shifting and then hitting with the front leg straight, the front knee bends and the weight shift continues through the swing. The back leg comes forward, causing the front knee to bend—opposite of what should happen during the swing (back leg bent, front leg stiff).

By lunging to hit the ball, the hitter loses the action of hitting against the frontside and loses power through the legs. Hitting against the frontside creates torque throughout the swing, giving maximum force behind the ball. Lunging also hinders the ability to hit off-speed pitches consistently and greatly affects pitch recognition and pitch selection because the hitter's head is moving so much.

Lunging stems from the hitter's natural desire to want to use the body's momentum to gain power. However, power should come from the body weight shifting and staying back, not by lunging.

Derek Lohr

Often, lunging is related to some other problem. It can be mechanical, like casting and dropping the barrel head. Or it can be non-mechanical, like poor bat speed, power, or timing. If the hitter casts the hands or drops the barrel head down, the swing will be longer and slower to the ball. He has to start the swing earlier, which affects his timing. Lunging may be the hitter's way of trying to catch up to the ball and hit the ball on the barrel. It's a similar effect when the hitter's bat speed is slow. The hitter has to find a way to get the barrel on the ball, so he lunges to compensate.

To fix the problem of lunging, I start with mechanics. If the hitter continues to lunge at the ball, he may need to work on bat speed and timing. Teaching the hitter to hit against the frontside of the body, and to stay back after the body weight shifts, also may help. To recognize that a hitter is lunging is half the battle. The key is to understand why.

Dipping

"Dipping" is another obvious mechanical issue best described as an uppercut to the ball, where the back shoulder or hands drop as the hitter swings through. I even had a grandparent tell me, "If Johnny would stop dipping he could hit the dang ball!"

I've worked with many hitters who have had this dipping motion in their swing, including some who have had some success at the plate. However, dipping allows hitters to have success only with specific pitches and speeds. For example, they're usually better curveball hitters because the uppercut action stays on the same plane of the ball longer. However, every hitter who swings this way struggles with certain pitches and pitch locations, especially fastballs inside and high fastballs. He may occasionally hit the ball hard, but will be inconsistent. If the hitter is limited in their hitting abilities because of swing mechanics, a change must be made.

By far, the most common reason why hitters dip is because of the ever-enticing home run. This is a great example of the mentality causing specific swing flaws to happen.

Another reason a hitter might dip is because he has a tendency to hit the ball too far back in the hitting zone and not out front. When this happens, the swing must "dip" to get square to the ball. The hitter's hands make a circular motion going back, down, and then back up to try and catch up to the ball that is being contacted almost behind their body. The shoulder leans back along with the rest of the body in an effort to hit the ball on the barrel of the bat. All of this may happen because of bad pitch recognition or just trying to hit the ball too deep. I see this when a coach is working with hitters on hitting the ball to the opposite field. The hitter tries to hit every pitch too deep and slowly develops a dip in his swing. I agree that we should teach hitters to let the ball travel, but in order to correctly hit the ball the opposite way, the hitter still must contact the ball out by the frontside of the body. Also, remember to be careful in making all hitters do the same things. The last thing some hitters need is to be forced to hit the ball to the opposite field!

Most of the time, fixing a dipping motion begins with working on the hitter's mentality, driving home the idea that the hitter doesn't have to hit a home run with every swing. It's hard, because most hitters who dip love to try for the fences. I also stress the importance of consistency in the swing, and how dipping doesn't give the hitter a chance to hit all pitches.

If the hitter is contacting the ball too deep, I tell them they're not allowed to hit the ball to the opposite field. The hitter usually responds by throwing his hands forward quicker, contacting the ball more out by their front foot and getting rid of the dipping action.

These are a few reasons why a hitter may be dipping. In my experience, most hitters don't swing like this all of the time, just when they are going for the long ball!

Wrapping

"Wrapping" happens when the hitter's hands load too far back behind the head, creating a twisting motion. The bat "wraps" around behind the head, causing the swing path to the ball to get long and circular. When the hands start the swing from behind the head, the hitter will struggle to consistently get the bat to the ball quick enough.

Most hitters wrap for one of two reasons: they want more power, and they're not loading in their legs. When a hitter is wrapping, an upper-body "twisting" motion usually takes place. The twist is an effort to get the hands back farther to create more torque and power in the swing. As a result, the hitter will load with all upper body, leaving the legs out of the equation.

In doing this, the hitter also creates a longer swing to get to the ball and doesn't use his legs for power. Getting the hands back away from the face may help generate more power, but twisting to do so would be counterproductive. Instead, the hands should go straight back in the load, generating the wanted power and also keeping the hand path to the ball shorter. If the hand path to the ball cannot get to contact quick enough, it won't matter how much power is being generated because it will not get used.

In teaching players not to wrap the bat, be careful not to mistake bat wrap for the bat angle. When the hitter gets into his stance, the bat should start slightly angled toward the head, but not wrapped behind the head. Even during the load, that bat angle should stay where it is, but might look like it is wrapping. This is where some coaches get confused. The barrel head of the bat, in the load, should be somewhere close to over the hitter's head. The problem of wrapping occurs when the hitter loads, keeping that same bat angle, but drops the barrel head back behind his neck instead of keeping it up above his head. Focus on loading straight back, more with the legs, but keeping the correct bat angle.

Paul Gran

Non-Mechanical Issues

Now you know the mechanical issues that I see everyday and how to identify them. What happens when no major mechanical problems in the swing need fixing? It means the hitter is ready to step up his game and really start learning how to hit.

For a hitter who has pretty good swing mechanics, identifying what to work on should come directly from the results on the field. Knowing if the hitter is popping up, hitting ground balls, pulling balls, hitting to the opposite field, swinging at good pitches, swinging at bad pitches, letting good pitches go by—all of this information will point to what he should work on. Understanding what causes these results on the field is an important step to figuring out what the hitter truly needs.

I'm going to give some reasons why these results on the field may happen when we know that the hitter is mechanically sound. Let's begin with the hitter's vision.

Pitch selection and pitch recognition: Every result on the field can be attributed to bad pitch selection. If the hitter is constantly swinging at bad pitches, he won't be able to hit the ball hard with any consistency. The strike zone is there for a reason, and swing mechanics are designed so the hitter can hit the ball in that specific area. Hitters who swing at strikes are always better than hitters who don't! If the hitter has bad pitch selection, it will result in undesirable outcomes on the field.

Bad pitch selection is tied to pitch recognition. If the hitter doesn't recognize the pitch very well, the most common results are swinging at bad pitches, rolling over off-speed pitches, and being consistently late on fastballs. The hitter's vision is extremely important when it comes to success on the field. All great hitters have awesome vision, which gives them an unbelievable ability to recognize pitches.

Matt Stefansson

Fear of the ball: Being afraid of getting hit by a pitch is a common problem, especially for younger hitters. When a hitter is fearful of the ball, swing mechanics do not matter! The batter will tend to take a lot of pitches, step out with his front foot, and if he ever does make contact, it's usually to the opposite field. I've seen hitters with awesome swings totally freeze in game situations because of the fear of being hit by the pitch. To work on this, my goal is to change the hitter's mentality. Instead of dwelling on the negative—"Please don't hit me! Please don't hit me! Please don't hit me!"—the hitter should step up to the plate thinking, "I am going to crush the ball!"

Most hitters eventually grow out of this fear (if not, they end up pitching!). Our job as coaches is to encourage them as much as possible and not to give up on them. I've worked with a couple of hitters in particular who were so scared of the ball that they would backpedal out of the box (no joke—moonwalk out of the box!). In time, something clicked in their heads and they are now some of the best hitters I have ever worked with, well on the way to playing at the college level.

When a hitter is afraid of the ball, it takes time to fix. Fear always controls the mindset of the hitter. Until the fear goes away, the hitter will never have the opportunity to hit to his full potential.

Timing: Timing is one of the most important aspects in all of hitting. In fact, if an advanced hitter is struggling, it's the first thing I look at.

Timing is best described as all of the movements of the swing working together to achieve consistent contact with the ball in the hitting zone. Bad timing can cause any of the major swing flaws to happen, while good timing can help fix any of those problems. This is why it is so important.

There are four mechanical parts of the swing that most commonly affect timing: loading early enough, shifting the body weight, getting the front foot down quick enough, and hitting against the frontside. When these movements work together properly and consistently, the hitter has a better chance to contact the ball on time.

Loading too late always forces the hitter to try and catch up to the ball, which leads to major mechanical problems. If the body weight of the hitter shifts too early, it may cause them to lunge or contact the ball too far out front. If the weight shifts too late, the hands will drag behind the body, causing the contact to be too far back in the hitting zone.

Getting the front foot down early is a common misconception in hitting. I may make a hitter get his front foot down earlier to try and fix specific mechanical elements, but the hitter does not have to get his front foot down early, he has to get it down quickly!

If the stride foot does not get down quick enough, the hips and hands can't get to the ball quickly enough. When the front heel drops, the backside rotates, helping the hitter hit against the frontside. If the hitter does not hit against the frontside, lunging will occur, directly affecting the timing of the swing.

Other non-mechanical issues may lead to bad results on the field. I will address bat speed, confidence, adjustments, approach, and mentality in later chapters. There is always a reason why hitters do what they do, and it may have nothing to do with how they swing the bat. Don't be too quick to jump to mechanical conclusions to assess a hitter's weaknesses. Sometimes, the mechanical swing flaws you can see are caused by something that's not mechanical at all.

The Circle Effect

No matter the outcome when a hitter steps up to the plate, in every case there is a cause to the effect. Whether he strikes out, pops up, rolls over, gets jammed, etc., you can point to a specific reason for the result (pitch selection, casting, timing, lunging, etc.).

In my day-to-day experience teaching hitting, every hitter I see can do something to improve. Some obviously have more to work on than others. Advanced hitters may need to focus on their plan and approach, pitch recognition, and fine-tuning mechanics. Beginner or intermediate hitters can work on basic mechanical elements of their individual swings. Whatever level the hitter is at, from Little League to the Major Leagues, the "Circle Effect" is the best description for the causes of the effects we see on the diamond.

Picture a circle in your mind. Inside that circle is the hitter's main problem (the effect or result on the field). On the circle are all of the little things that may cause this problem to occur. As the hitter addresses those smaller problems on the circle, the big issue inside the circle will eventually get fixed as well. The interesting thing here is that most of the time, the little things on the circle cause the other little things on the circle to happen. As hitter improves on certain aspects, others will naturally improve as well.

Here is a good example of the circle effect. Let's say there is a hitter whose main problem is hitting a lot of ground balls to his pull side. He occasionally hits balls hard, but most are rolled-over ground balls that turn into outs. Also, the hitter pulls the ball almost every time contact is made and rarely hits the ball to the opposite field. In analyzing the swing, there are several things, all working together, to cause this effect:

The hitter's timing is off because he starts his load too late. This makes his hands cast and get long to the ball, which prevents him from getting extension through the ball. The backside over-rotates, the head pulls off, and the hands end up rolling over. The hitter may lunge and contact the ball too far out front, which slows his bat speed. All of these specific things go on the circle in no particular order. So now we have the effect (inside the circle) and some of the things that cause this effect (on the circle).

The Circle Effect is a way to establish the hitter's problem, list the particular elements that contribute to the problem, and help you identify what this individual really needs to succeed. The hardest part is identifying the effect, especially with advanced hitters. Identifying the causes is no easy task either. As a coach, take your time and make sure the analysis of the cause and effect is correct. If this analysis is correct, the hitter can begin to fix what causes his main weaknesses on the field.

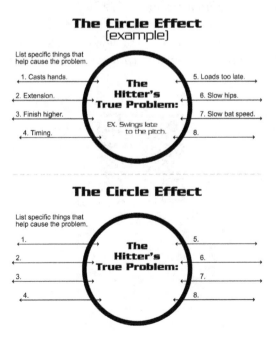

The Circle Effect
(example)

List specific things that help cause the problem.

1. Casts hands.
2. Extension.
3. Finish higher.
4. Timing.

The Hitter's True Problem:
EX. Swings late to the pitch.

5. Loads too late.
6. Slow hips.
7. Slow bat speed.
8.

The Circle Effect

List specific things that help cause the problem.

1.
2.
3.
4.

The Hitter's True Problem:

5.
6.
7.
8.

Bottom of the 2nd

When you're teaching hitting, it's important to analyze what a hitter really needs. Identifying the weaknesses of an individual hitter starts with knowing what the common swing flaws look like. Recognizing these flaws is crucial to a hitter's development, and helps in fixing the hitter's biggest problems at the plate. However, there is a lot more to it. There is always a reason why these mechanical flaws happen in hitting, and the answer is not always mechanical. Do not to jump to conclusions that all swing flaws happen because of mechanical reasons. This is a common misconception in teaching hitting. The Circle Effect can help you understand how everything mechanical and non-mechanical works together in hitting.

After figuring out the hitter's true problems, fixing those problems takes time. Don't work on too many things at once. Because most swing flaws cause other swing flaws to happen, if the hitter works on fixing certain issues, other issues will naturally improve as well! If the hitter can identify what causes his negative results on the field, and then fix these issues, he will find more consistent success at the plate. This will also allow him to advance into learning the aspects he needs to become a "hitter." Bat speed, mentality, making adjustments, and approach are the next steps in this development, but to get to this level, we must be able to identify and fix the hitter's on field problems.

—End of the 2nd

Teaching hitting isn't as easy as knowing what the swing should look like, but giving the hitter what he really needs!

The Ultimate Game Changer DVD Series + the 9 Innings of Hitting

See the concepts from *9 Innings of Hitting* at work in *The Ultimate Game Changer,* a DVD series produced by the coaches at Rijo Athletics. These high-definition DVDs feature three hours of drills and analysis in a fun, upbeat, engaging atmosphere. In my opinion, it's the best video series available and a great companion to the *9 Innings of Hitting.* Make your training exciting! *The Ultimate Game Changer* is available at Amazon and at rijoathletics.com.

Chapter 2

3rd Inning

The Importance of Bat Speed

How to increase bat speed and hit the ball farther

A 90-mph fastball will reach home plate in less than half a second. Within this tiny amount of time, a hitter must recognize the speed of the pitch, spin of the ball, and location of the pitch. His brain must decide whether to swing, and then relay more messages telling the body what to do. All of this happens before the hitter actually starts his swing. Now do you see why hitting is the hardest thing to do in all of sports?

With so little time to react, you can see why bat speed is a key component to the overall success of the hitter.

Bat speed is the velocity of the bat to and through the hitting zone. Good bat speed enables the hitter to let the ball travel a little bit longer into the hitting zone, giving him extra time to recognize the pitch and decide whether or not to swing. This extra time equates to several one-hundredths of a second, an eternity in the pitch-selection and pitch-recognition process. A hitter who is able to see the pitch longer and can get his barrel head to the ball faster can start his swing later. With the limited amount of time the hitter has to make decisions, quicker bat speed gives the hitter a better opportunity for success.

Besides allowing the hitter more time to see the ball before he swings, bat speed generates more power. For every 1 mph a hitter gains in bat speed, the ball will travel approximately 3 to 5 feet farther. Show me a hitter who would not like to hit the ball harder and farther and I will tell you he is flat-out lying. *All* hitters would love to hit the ball with greater force and distance.

The intent of this chapter is to show you ways to increase bat speed for all ages and skill levels. I assure you that hitters who use these proven techniques will swing at better pitches, be on time with good fastballs, hit the ball harder and farther, and, most of all, the hitter will be more confident at the plate. I have consistently seen that creating more bat speed and power helps tremendously in the overall success of the hitter. Developing more bat speed helps to build confidence, which plays a key part in being a great hitter.

Understanding the importance of bat speed is a big step toward the overall development of a hitter. To gain bat speed, the hitter must have a combination of the right mindset, explosive mechanics, specific bat speed tools, and proper strength training. If the hitter commits to doing these things, there should be a gain in bat speed by at least 5 to 10 mph, which could equate to an extra 25 to 50 feet of extra distance on the batted ball. If there is no significant jump in bat speed after doing these things, I suggest you contact me at Rijo Athletics and I will personally get it out of you.

Mentality

A hitter's mindset greatly impacts bat speed. The mentality a hitter needs at the plate will be covered in great detail in the next chapter. For now, I will only get into what is required to maximize bat speed and power.

First of all, a hitter should not *try* to hit the ball; he should *expect* to hit the ball. I call it the "trying" mentality. It is the mindset of *trying* to hit the ball that greatly affects the hitter's ability to generate maximum bat speed. It might be the fear of failure, or a lack of success, but whatever the reason, it has a direct impact on the hitter's bat speed.

Let me explain. When a hitter goes to the plate with the "trying" mentality, his whole focus is on not swinging and missing and his bat speed almost always slows down. The hitter who *expects* to hit the ball has the mentality to attack it. This expectation of hitting the ball, even if he swings and misses, creates the mindset the hitter needs to maximize his bat speed. I heard an awesome slogan a while back that has stuck with me over the years: "swing hard in case you hit it." This has never been more true in explaining this "expect to hit it" mentality, especially for younger hitters. If the hitter *expects* to hit the ball, rather than *tries* to hit the ball, a visible difference in their bat speed will be seen.

The aggressive mindset of attacking the ball and being ready to hit also influences the production of bat speed. Since there is no time for thought in recognizing pitches, this mindset makes the hitter maximize whatever bat speed they have in them. When a hitter uses this controlled aggression at the plate, I call it, "swinging the bat like a man" (or "*whoa*-man" for my fast-pitch girls). The attitude of taking a "man hack" at the ball helps to make the hitter's bat speed aggressive, quick and explosive. The right mentality in the batter's box will let the hitter's swing mechanics work to increase bat speed.

Rhythm/Getting the Hands Ready to Hit

Every good hitter has some kind of movement in his setup and stance. This movement is called rhythm. Rhythm helps the hitter stay loose and relaxed as he prepares to aggressively swing the bat. Hitters also use rhythm for timing in the load.

Andy Littlefield

As you've learned, the main purpose of the load is for timing. It also helps bat speed and power. The load helps to shift the body weight and gets the hips and hands ready to "explode" to the ball. One of the most important things in accelerating bat speed is getting the hands ready to hit. Coaches overlook this because they focus on teaching pretty swing mechanics rather than generating a quick and explosive swing.

The hands must have some movement during the load. Most of the time the hands will load back, cocking the top hand slightly in front of the bottom hand and creating a bat angle slightly toward the hitter's head. The hands may load slightly up or down depending on the hitter's preference, but the common goal is to get the hands ready to hit. This is important because when the hands have some movement, the hitter can feel the barrel head of the bat. If he can feel the barrel head of the bat, he can quickly drive the hands forward to the ball, creating a "whip" action, which is a big contributor to bat speed.

There are many different ways to teach a hitter to get the hands ready to hit. The only way that should not be allowed is when the hitter locks his hands into one spot without any movement whatsoever. This causes the shoulders to stiffen up, and the hitter to swing the bat with his shoulders instead of his hands. When the shoulders get involved, the hitter's bat speed will always be significantly slower than when the hands are doing the work. The hands need to have some kind of movement that gets the hitter ready to attack the ball.

Quick Hips

It's common to hear coaches tell hitters to have "quick hands" to the ball. You have probably heard this a million times. I would agree that quick hands tremendously help the hitter's overall success at the plate. However, quick

Vinny Catanzaro

hips is what creates quick hands. The hitter needs to focus on the hips and hands working together quickly to generate maximum power and bat speed. If the hitter can work on quick hip rotation, the hands will naturally speed up as well.

Hip rotation has always been a highly debated topic. In fact, it is one of the main disagreements between the linear and rotational hitting philosophies. Again, I think most coaches get consumed with what the hips are supposed to look like in the swing and forget how they help the hitter. The main reason for hip rotation is to generate more power and bat speed through the lower half of the body. This can only be done if the hips rotate quickly. The quicker the hips, the more explosive the swing gets. When a hitter speeds up the lower body hip rotation, it speeds the hands up as well, and allows the barrel head to get to the ball quicker with more force behind it.

Since the hitter has such a small amount of time to react to the pitch, quick hips also plays a huge role in pitch recognition. The quicker the hips are, the longer the hitter can let the ball travel, enabling better pitch recognition. Remember, to see the ball even a few hundredths of a second longer before the hitter has to swing is a tremendous advantage, and speeding up the hip rotation allows this to happen. Learning how to use the hips quickly and explosively is one of the most important factors in helping the hitter generate more bat speed and power.

Bat Whip/Top Hand Whip/Speed Up Swing

Everyone knows that the bat is a stiff object, and stiff objects cannot truly be whipped. The bat "whipping" to the ball is more of an analogy of what the hitter's hands should feel like when he swings the bat. If you were to roll up a towel and try to snap it, the only way the snapping action can occur is through the wrists and hands. This is the same with bat whip. The only way bat whip can occur is through the wrists and hands.

The reason why bat whip is so important stems from the misconception that extension is a pushing motion. *The hitter should never push the bat to the ball.* This pushing motion gets taught to hitters because coaches get overly concerned with the hitter "rolling over" and unintentionally exaggerate pushing the bat to get more extension. This hinders the hitter's ability to maximize power and bat speed. When the hitter pushes his hands through the ball in an effort to get more extension, the top hand does not whip and the bat speed slows down through the swing. If the hitter learns how to whip the bat, instead of pushing the bat through the ball, he can speed the barrel head up through the extension and finish of the swing. This creates a whip action with the bat, generating better bat speed.

The top hand plays a key role. The top hand must whip, not push, to get extension through the ball. This means that at contact, the hitter's top hand creates extension by whipping the barrel head through the ball. Coaches need to be careful when teaching exactly what the top hand does during the swing because if it is not explained properly, the hitter may develop a tendency to roll the hands over too soon. Top hand whip helps the hitter to forcefully speed up the swing during the contact, extension, and finish, which is crucial in the development of bat speed.

One common thing that prevents the hitter from generating maximum power and bat speed to the ball is when the swing slows down at contact. If the hitter consistently slows down his bat at contact, a tremendous amount of power is lost. Younger hitters sometimes have the tendency to let the ball almost completely stop their bat at contact. Advanced hitters who find themselves slowing down their swings usually do so because they are making contact too far out front. Hitters need to train themselves to always finish their swing aggressively. An aggressive finish helps speed up the bat at contact, which is mandatory if a player wants more power. It also forces the hitter to let the ball travel into the hitting zone, because you cannot speed up your swing and finish aggressively if contact is being made too far out front.

In all my years of teaching hitting, I have used many ways to generate more bat speed. In most cases, bat whip best explains what needs to happen when the hands drive through the ball. The top hand whipping through the extension, the barrel head speeding up at contact, and finishing aggressively all contribute to enabling the bat to whip through the ball. Incorporating these helpful ways to produce better bat speed into the hitter's swing will result in more power output on the field.

Bat Weights

There is a huge debate about whether bat weights can increase a hitter's bat speed. The sports-science people of the world claim that bat weights or heavier bats do not improve bat speed, and guess what? It may come as a surprise but I am not going to even try to argue against them. However, I am definitely not letting them off the hook that easily. What these "sports scientists" don't understand is what weighted bats do for players both physically and mentally.

In my opinion, it would be stupid not to use some sort of weighted bat, especially with players from Little League to high school. I definitely recommend using bat weights more during the off-season and using the hitter's normal bat during the season, but it depends on what the player really needs. *It is completely OK to swing a weighted bat during the season.* If you disagree, then why does almost every big-leaguer swing one on deck before every at-bat? The answer is simple. Besides helping the hitter loosen up, it provides a confidence factor by making his bat feel lighter.

My own observable, repeatable, and measurable science over the past decade tells me this: hitters who use bat weights consistently and properly will see an increase in bat speed due to the overall strengthening of the hands, wrists, and forearms. More importantly, their confidence will increase by swinging a heavier bat. Bat weights also force hitters to learn how to power through a ball, rather than just hit it, because of the momentum created by the weight of the bat. Nearly every hitter I see who swings a weighted bat gains bat speed once they get their normal bat back in their hands. If they don't actually see an increase in bat speed, they will *feel* an increase in bat speed, which is probably more important. Who really knows if bat weights alone can increase a hitter's bat speed? All I can say is that in my experience, using bat weights with proper supervision does something to a hitter's mentality and confidence that can't be measured by normal scientific standards.

Strength Training

Strength training is what separates a player from being able to compete at a high level or not. Now, more than ever, if an athlete does not commit to getting stronger, he will eventually be surpassed by those who do. If there is one thing that I regret the most in my playing career, it would be my lack of determination to lift weights. At the time, no one told me about the importance of strength training, or the benefits if I committed myself to it. Looking back, this was a detriment to my overall development as a hitter. By not working hard in the weight room, I left a big "what if?" regarding my full potential.

However, I believe that all things happen for a reason. Based on my experience, I can now inform kids why they must make strength training a priority. I understand what it can do both physically and mentally for a hitter. I see the results of hard work every day. Knowing how weight training can improve his performance will hopefully give the hitter a desire to do it. I don't what anyone to look back at his career and say, "I wish I would have worked harder in the weight room."

There are many reasons why athletes must take strength training seriously. It helps to prevent injury, increase flexibility, and develop endurance. Specifically, it can help the hitter generate more power and explosiveness, faster bat speed, and better control of specific movements during the swing. Strength training also brings out a level of commitment, helping the hitter develop the work ethic necessary for success.

However, there's more to it than that. Strength training is *huge* for the overall development of a hitter's mentality. A player who has the desire to push himself in the weight room will build confidence, toughness, and learn how to battle through adversity. In most cases, it is more important for hitters to get serious in the weight room for the mental aspects rather than just for pure strength.

These are important reasons why strength training should be mandatory for hitters who want to step up their game. That being said, a hitter should not even think about weight training until his swing mechanics are consistent. All the strength in the world does not matter if the swing mechanics are bad.

The age to start strength training is about 14 years old, or when the player enters high school. This is when I allow hitters with sound mechanical swings to begin lifting weights as long as it is done properly. Do not let kids 13 or younger lift weights. Younger players with a desire to work out should use their own body weight or light bands. Pushups, pull ups, squats, lunges, and other body-weight exercises are just as effective for building strength and do not carry the same risk of injury.

Baseball/Softball-Specific Strength Training

Specific exercises for baseball/softball have many benefits. The most important is shoulder protection. There are differences in how pitchers and position players should train (which I won't get into now), but if a player injures his throwing shoulder, he can't play. Baseball/softball-specific training will also strengthen areas of the body that help most with on-field movements. If the player understands which muscles generate quickness and explosiveness during these movements, he will be able to recognize what it takes to make his workouts more effective.

Finally, baseball/softball-specific weight training will give the athlete direction in the weight room. There are certain lifts that baseball/softball players should not do because they could hinder the way they throw the ball or swing the bat. There are lifts that greatly help these things as well.

In this section, I will talk about the dos and don'ts of lifting. I will cover how all of the major muscle groups are used in hitting, and what you need to know about developing them properly. I do not go into great detail about form or technique; the idea here is to provide you with a basic approach to hitting-specific workouts.

The muscle groups that are used most during the swing are the legs, abs, back, triceps, and forearms. The shoulders, chest, and biceps aid in the overall power of the swing, but do not play as big of a role. The legs load, shift the body weight, balance, and control the hip rotation. The abs and back pull the hands to the ball. At contact, the forearms provide the force and the triceps give the extension through the ball. This is a quick description of how the muscles function throughout the swing, and how different muscle groups are used more than others.

The frequency of weight training depends on the age of the player and time of year. Younger athletes who are just beginning should not lift more than three times a week, while more advanced athletes can train four to five times a week. The legs, back, and triceps can be trained up to two times a week, while the shoulders, chest, and biceps should only be worked once a week. Abs and forearms can be worked more if desired. In the off-season, workouts should be more frequent with the intention of gaining size and strength. In-season, the focus should be on maintaining this strength and trying to get at least three workouts done each week. This is all dependent on the individual's desire and work ethic.

Nick Aucott

Proper technique makes training more productive and reduces the risk of injury. All exercises should begin from an athletic position, with the knees slightly bent, chest up, and shoulders back. Posture is important: good posture in the weight room equates to good posture in the batter's box, which allows the body to function better throughout the swing. All lifts should be performed with a full range of motion, which enables the player to gain strength but also retain flexibility. The athlete should always control the weight, and not allow the weight to control him. This makes the muscles work harder, putting less stress on the joints, and produces a safer, more efficient workout. With advanced athletes, certain fast-twitch exercises can improve explosiveness; however, these lifts must be controlled. Also, adding certain balancing movements to lifts will enable hitters to simulate a balanced, explosive swing.

If all of these functions are done properly, the only thing left is to lift hard. This can only get accomplished if the individual lifts with a purpose. I see too many people in the weight room who aren't sweating or breathing heavily. They exercise to get it done rather than to get stronger. I think a lot of this is due to the "functional training" approach that is common among personal trainers these days. It is all about the functions of the movements rather than the athlete's mentality and determination. Let me tell you this: *all* lifts should be naturally functional. Quite honestly, I'm tired of hearing about functional training because it overlooks some of the most important mental aspects of training.

The only way to gain size and strength is to fatigue the muscle, so the goal for every set should be to work that specific muscle to failure. This is a mental choice that the athlete needs to make when lifting: it's either *one more rep,* or *I give up.* The athlete must push himself beyond his normal limits and not focus so much on how to be more "functional." Technique and functionality are important, and I'm not saying that hitters need to become bodybuilders. However, to become physically and mentally better at the plate, hitters need to challenge themselves mentally in their weight-room workouts.

Stretching/Flexibility

Muscle length plus muscle strength equals hitting power. Hitters need to build strength and flexibility to improve bat speed and power. Flexibility, like anything else in hitting, is something the player must work at. However, you only get out of stretching what you put into it. Don't overlook the importance of stretching properly.

Players should spend at least 10 to 15 minutes before every workout or practice on improving their flexibility in both the upper and lower body. Muscles are easier to stretch when they are warm, so start with a light jog. Then, no matter what stretch is being performed, it should always be held for a minimum of 20 seconds. Static, controlled stretching is the most common and safest way to stretch, but there are also some dynamic stretches that are beneficial as well.

Poor flexibility affects a swing the most when the hitter is tied up in the shoulder/chest area. I work with a lot of strong kids who play football and baseball and train hard in the weight room. They do lifts specifically for football, like heavy bench press, power cleans, and shrugs. I do not recommend these lifts to hitters. The real problem is not the exercises but how the athletes perform them, as well as their poor commitment to stretching and staying flexible. By not taking stretching seriously, these hitters will normally be stiff in their shoulders and chest. They have to swing the bat around their chest, which creates a longer swing and a slower bat speed. Good flexibility, however, allows the hitter's swing movements to be as explosive as possible.

Core

There is an overemphasis on the core (the abs and lower back) in strength training for baseball/softball today. Coaches are so focused on getting the player's core stronger that they neglect the rest of the body. Don't get me wrong, the hitter's core plays a major role in bat speed development, and core work should be done consistently. However, when the sole purpose of strength training is to build up the abs and low back, the hitter does not receive the full benefits of weight training. Besides missing out on the obvious overall strength and power other muscle groups contribute to the swing, "core only" workouts do not help develop the hitter's mentality. A player who commits to giving a max effort in the weight room will build a tough mindset and confidence that will transfer into their approach at the plate. This mentality cannot be created if the hitter only focuses on core workouts.

Hitting-specific core workouts are designed to simulate the hitting action and help generate more power and bat speed. The main exercise should consist of rotational trunk twists. There are various ways to do trunk twists, but no matter what exercise is being done it should be performed in a balanced and explosive manner. A strong core is important for the overall balance, power, and bat speed of a hitter's swing. Make sure the hitter does not focus on core workouts alone. Hitting-specific strength training should not be limited to one area of the body!

Shoulders

The shoulders are the most important muscle group to be careful with when lifting weights. Remember, if your shoulder is injured, you cannot throw. If you cannot throw, you cannot play baseball/softball.

With shoulder workouts, the emphasis should be on making sure the exercises are being done properly and for the right reasons. The shoulders can help or hinder the hitter's ability to get extension through the ball. Shoulder strength and flexibility allow the swing to be shorter and quicker to the ball, while shoulder stiffness causes the swing to get longer and slower. So the focus should be on creating a controlled, complete range of motion that will help increase flexibility and protect the shoulder from weight room injuries.

There are some specific shoulder lifts that need to be done with caution. Any type of overhead press puts the shoulder at risk if the weight is too heavy. Shoulder presses are OK for hitters as long as they are done under control and with moderate to light weight. Shoulder presses done correctly, with the arms fully extending over the head, will help with the hitter's extension during the swing. Power cleans put so much stress on the rotator cuff that, to me, they're not even worth attempting because of the chance of injury. If a hitter chooses to do power cleans, keep the weight lighter for the sake of protecting his career. Heavy upright rows and shrugs, done without a full range of motion, have the tendency lock up the hitter's shoulders. We already know that locked-up shoulders create slower swings, so make sure these lifts are done with the intent of creating strength while keeping flexibility.

The common thing with all of these specific lifts is to be careful not to go too heavy, and to control the weight using a full range of motion. All other shoulder exercises are OK to do as long as common sense and good judgment is used. Lift shoulders hard, but lift shoulders smart. An injury to your throwing shoulder could cause an unwanted, premature retirement!

Chest

All guys who lift weights want a bigger chest. "Beach muscles" are highly desirable for us prideful males, and having big pecs is where it's at! Anybody who has ever lifted weights, especially in his younger days, knows that bench pressing is the pathway to manhood. Ask any young athlete what his max bench press is and I am sure he will tell you with pride.

With the chest, the main focus when lifting should be on gaining strength, but keeping flexibility (see a common theme here?). Unfortunately, the only lift that I strongly discourage is the straight-bar bench press. Let me tell you why. If bench pressing is done correctly, with the right amount of weight, there should not be a

Zach Vander Hoek

problem with doing it. But as I stated before, bench pressing is a pride thing. Athletes who bench press will sacrifice form in the hope of increasing their max. This is the first problem; young athletes bench press to max out and strive for only one repetition. Consistent low repetitions in lifting the chest will cause a big decrease in flexibility.

Another problem is they do not focus on technique. They do things like bounce the weight off of their chest, or arch their back. This puts extra, unwanted pressure on the rotator cuff, and risks serious injury to the shoulder. In my opinion, the biggest problem with straight-bar benching is that because the hands have to be spaced far apart on the bar, you can't have a full range of motion. Because the arms do not fully extend at the top, this consistent movement hinders the hitter's extension during his swing. All of these problems with the bench press give good reason for not doing it at all. However, if a player bench presses occasionally without prideful intentions, and with proper technique, it is not going to hurt him. Tell him to put his pride away before it costs him a career.

Instead of straight-bar bench pressing, hitters should do more dumbbell and cable work. Dumbbell or cable presses are more effective for hitters because it gives more freedom throughout the shoulder area and allows for the extra range of motion at the top of the lift. Dumbbell or cable flys are exceptional ways to increase strength and flexibility through the chest area and front of the shoulder. There are many other chest exercises that can be done in the weight room that will greatly improve a hitter's bat speed and power. By doing these hitting-specific lifts, the player will be able take his hard work in the weight room and transfer it effectively onto the field.

For baseball, a bigger chest does not help the swing. In fact, in most cases, it slows down the swing. A hitter who has to swing around a big, bulky, inflexible chest will have too long of a swing to consistently compete against advanced pitching. The chest muscles do not directly contribute to improving a hitter's bat speed, but they do help produce strength and power, which generate force through the ball. Because the chest connects into the front of the shoulder, using extreme caution in your workouts is advised.

Back

The hitter's back is highly involved in the overall function of the swing. Since the swing is a rotational movement, the lower back needs to be strong to handle the repetitive twisting motion. The lat muscles help to pull the hands to the ball and also are used through the extension of the swing. Good posture is important in hitting and is improved by lifting the back with the correct form and technique. Back workouts are also important for gaining forearm and grip strength. Any time a pulling motion is done, the hands, wrists, and forearms are used to hold onto the weight. This fatigues the forearms and strengthens the hands, which gives the hitter more bat whip through the hitting zone.

Strengthening the back not only benefits bat speed, but also helps to prevent injury. From what I have seen, back injuries are the most common injuries because swinging the bat puts a lot of stress on the back. A strong back is necessary if the hitter wants to develop better bat speed, keep good posture, and prevent injuries.

There are several muscle groups that together make up the large area of the back. It is important to do different exercises, from all different angles, to make sure the whole back is being strengthened and not just one

Kody Sanders

isolated area. Various types of lat pull downs, rows, and reverse flys will hit all areas of the back, ensuring total back strengthening. However, although the lower back is used for all these lifts, the importance of isolated low-back exercises is often overlooked. Remember, becoming a better hitter involves swinging the bat over and over. Thousands upon thousands of aggressive hacks will take place during a hitter's career, so strengthening the lower back should be taken seriously. Lower back exercises, commonly called "supermans," should be performed at least twice a week, with repetitions in the 20 to 30 range. Lower-back exercises are extremely important for hitters and need to be integrated into back workouts to strengthen the entire back.

When strengthening the back, there are a few things that help maximize the workouts because the back is the hardest muscle group to train. The reason why it is so hard is improper form and technique. All back exercises are done by pulling weight toward the body. If the lift is not done incorrectly, the athlete will think he is doing back exercises, but will be putting more fatigue on the bicep instead. This happens when the athlete initiates the lift by pulling with his arms and not his back. To start all back exercises, the chest must be upright, with the shoulders back. The first movement in the lift should be to pinch the shoulder blades together and start the pulling motion with the back. If the athlete can learn to pull the weight with the back, he will effectively isolate the back muscles during the lift and create better postural mechanics.

One lift that should be done with caution is the lat pull down behind the head. I would prefer that baseball/softball players not do it because it puts the shoulder and neck in an awkward position and adds unwanted stress to the rotator cuff. All other lifts involving the back are OK to do as long as the weight is being controlled and the pulling motion is done with a full range of motion and proper form.

By training the back, the hitter will improve posture, bat speed to the ball, extension through the swing, and forearm and grip strength. It will also help prevent common back injuries that occur due to the toll that repetitively swinging the bat will put on the body. I have seen many really good hitters have to quit playing because of back injuries. It is unfortunate, but in some cases, it could have been prevented if they had committed themselves to doing the necessary things in the weight room.

Biceps

The bicep is another beach muscle that guys train too much with hopes of looking good. The baseball/softball athlete should work the biceps like he would the chest: very carefully. The bicep connects into both the shoulder and the elbow, which are vital for throwing the ball. A bicep injury can be as debilitating as injuring the elbow or shoulder. This puts extreme importance on form and control when doing bicep curls. Since the main function of the bicep during the swing is to fully straighten out, hitters need to understand the most important things in training them properly.

There are no specific bicep lifts that hitters should not do. The curl is the foundation of all bicep exercises. Two of the most common lifting errors for curls are: 1) not controlling the weight on the downward part of the lift; and 2) not extending the arms fully at the bottom of the lift. When heavier weight is let down too fast in the downward part of the lift, it can cause injury to the bicep. If the arms do not get a full range of motion at the bottom of the lift, it consistently shortens the range in the repetitions. In the long run, the hitter will develop a bigger, but shorter, less flexible bicep. The lack flexibility and extension in the bicep can transfer into the hitter's swing.

Strong biceps are important to the overall power of the swing and need to be trained just as hard as any other muscle in the body. They should be trained no more than once a week, with the emphasis being on gaining strength and length to produce more swing extension. If you play baseball, biceps need to be trained for the swing, not for the beach.

Triceps

The primary job of the triceps during the swing is to fully extend the player's arms. When the triceps get strong extension through the ball, the result is more force behind the swing. There are various exercises that the athlete can do to produce more power, bat speed and flexibility. The one exercise that hitters need to be extra careful with is the dip. For some, the bar dip or bench dip sometimes puts uncomfortable pressure on the front of the shoulder. If the player feels any discomfort, he should stop because there are so many other lifts that they can deliver the same result. If he can do dips without discomfort, it is a great lift for triceps strength and shoulder flexibility.

To gain maximum hitting benefits in triceps workouts, the most important thing to focus on is to fully extend the arms. Whether the athlete is doing pushups, pushdowns, overhead extensions, or any other possible triceps lift, the goal should be to get full extension when the arms straighten. If the lift is done with the correct form and a full range of motion it will directly benefit the hitter's power on the field. The triceps can be trained a couple times week, and are the major extension makers of the swing.

Forearms

A hitter must have strong hands, wrists, and forearms to swing the bat quickly and explosively. The grip strength on the bat at the point of contact determines how much force the bat whip will create through the ball. Hitters who don't have strong forearms are unable to forcefully speed the bat head up through the ball. The velocity of the ball makes the bat "give" at contact instead of powering through. If the hitter's forearms and grip are stronger, he will have the ability to generate the desired bat whip to and through the ball. This maximizes the player's bat speed and gives him a better chance of strong contact with the ball.

Forearm lifts need to be performed with more repetition, usually in the 20 to 30 range, because it takes longer to fatigue those specific muscles. This is great for developing a tougher mentality because the burning sensation felt when working forearms is like no other.

Forearms exercises are done by rolling the wrists up, down, in, or out. There are no specific exercises that the athlete should not do, but there should always a full range of motion. Grip-strengthening exercises will also help the hitter whip the bat faster through the ball as well. These exercises consist of a "squeezing" motion with the hands. Squeezing tennis balls, racket balls, hand grips, etc., will strengthen the hands, wrists, and forearms to help improve the hitter's bat speed. Quick, fast-twitch movements can be done through this wrist rolling, or squeezing, action to help simulate the explosive whip created through the swing. Forearm and grip-strengthening exercises can be done consistently throughout the week—there is no real limit. If a hitter can battle through 5 to 10 minutes of these exercises on a consistent basis, the results will be phenomenal. He will be developing a tougher mindset and creating more power and bat speed all in just minutes a day!

Legs

The legs are responsible for generating balance and power through the lower half of the body. Strength in the hamstrings, quads, glutes, and calves is essential to an explosive and balanced lower half. Also, the hip flexors are important to the swing because of the emphasis placed on quicker hip rotation. When the lower- and upper-body strength are combined, the hitter's swing will perform at its highest potential.

The key to hitting specific leg workouts is literally a "balanced" approach. This means the athlete should lift all muscle groups hard, while focusing on balance and control. Isolated lifts that specifically strengthen and stretch the hip area are beneficial in keeping the hips quick and explosive during the swing. Plyometric exercises are also great for hitting. They are dynamic movements that involve using the athlete's own body weight for gaining strength and balance through the legs. Plyometric exercises should be integrated into leg workouts because they simulate the aggressive actions of the lower body during the swing.

Different kinds of squats, lunges, leg extensions, leg curls, and calf raises can be done to strengthen the legs. While there are no lifts that a hitter should not do for the legs, always remember to keep good posture, control the weight, and use a full range of motion. The main focus of leg workouts should be on gaining more flexibility through the hip area, and developing a more balanced and powerful lower body.

The hitter's legs are the foundation of the swing. If the foundation in the legs is strong, watch what the hitter can do!

The Steroid Era

Let me start by saying this: *I 100% disagree with the use of performance-enhancing drugs, or any illegal drug for that matter!*

The issue of steroids has been the center of conversation in the media for too long and I am glad that baseball is finally doing the necessary things to clean it up and move forward. We all make mistakes in our lives, but it is what we learn from them that makes us mature as people.

One of the main things I have learned through this time of widespread use of steroids in baseball is to tell the truth even when it hurts. I have a lot of respect for the players who have openly admitted to taking steroids, owned up to their bad decisions, and dealt with the consequences. Because of their truthfulness, these players

Josh Thompson

may have faced immediate scrutiny, but the situation will pass and we will soon forget that it ever happened. What is most unfortunate about the steroid era is that all of those players who stayed clean during this time will be forever linked to it, even when they played by the rules.

With all the negatives that steroids brought to baseball, the one big positive that came about because of it is the importance in strength training! The reason why I want to talk about this topic is not about the steroids themselves, but how important strength is in hitting. In the steroid era, there were *massive* numbers being put up. No one thought the home run record would ever be broken, yet it was shattered. It seemed like everyone was hitting 30 or more a year. Hitting was taken to a whole new level during this era. For those who chose to take them, steroids definitely provided a leg up on the competition. However, let me say that steroids do not make you a better hitter. They are not proven to help hand-eye coordination, pitch recognition, or vision. They help hitters increase strength, explosiveness, and allow for quicker muscle recovery. Because of the strength benefits from steroids, the hitter's bat speed increases which enables them to be quicker to the ball and gives them time to see the ball longer. This allows them to trust their bat speed more and gives the hitter more confidence in their abilities.

What players need to learn from the steroid era is that strength is a key element to better bat speed. The benefits of strength training are too important not to be taken seriously. The players who took steroids obviously knew the importance of strength in hitting, and unfortunately went to illegal measures to get an edge on the competition. In the new era of baseball, we still see the importance of strength. We can see that players spend a lot of time working hard in the weight room. The only difference is that now they are doing it legally, I hope!

Kory Longaker

Bottom of the 3rd

If a hitter wants to maximize his bat speed to its full potential, there are several things he must do. It starts with an aggressive mindset—a desire to attack the ball rather than just trying to make contact. When the hitter *expects* to hit the ball, the only thing left to think about is how hard.

How hard the ball is hit comes directly from bat speed powered by the hitter's physical strength and flexibility. There are numerous mechanical movements that, if done correctly, can increase bat speed. Unfortunately, these elements often get ignored because coaches pay too much attention to what the swing should look like and rarely give advice on how these mechanical things can help generate more bat speed.

To help create more power and bat speed, the hitter must make baseball/softball-specific strength training a priority. If the athlete understands the concept of hitting-specific lifting, and takes weight training seriously, he will have a better chance to compete against top-notch pitching. There are also various weighted bat tools that can increase bat speed if they are done consistently and monitored correctly. When a hitter combines an aggressive mindset, quicker mechanical movements, strength training, and the use of heavier bat weights, together it will enable their swing to perform at its highest potential.

Now that it's clear what it takes for a hitter to maximize his full potential bat speed, there are no excuses. If the hitter chooses not to work on the things that I have talked about in this chapter, the only one stopping him from playing at the next level is himself!

End of the Inning

There is such a limited time for decision-making in the pitch-recognition process. Quicker bat speed will give the hitter more opportunity for success.

Chapter 3

4th Inning
Hitting with a Purpose

What It Really Takes To Be a Great Hitter

I had the opportunity to play for one the best coaches of all time, Ed Cheff, at Lewis-Clark State College. Coach Cheff, who retired in 2010 after 34 seasons at L-C State, led his teams to an unprecedented 16 NAIA World Series titles, including the 1996 championship team that I played on. With a record of 1,705-430-2— a winning percentage of .800—he is the NAIA all-time leader in victories at one school and never had a season with fewer than 38 wins. More than 100 of his players at L-C State went on to play pro ball, and 14 made it to the big-leagues. Coach Cheff earned NAIA coach of the year eight times, was elected to the College Baseball Hall of Fame in 2012, and is simply in a league of his own when it comes to coaching.

I could go on about this man's accomplishments, but the point is to show you that what he teaches works. I am so thankful to have played for Ed Cheff because were it not for him, I would never have become the player I was. More importantly, I would not be the coach I am today. Many of my teaching principles come directly from what I learned from Coach Cheff, especially when it comes to the hitter's mentality.

Every team must have good players in order to consistently win, and Coach Cheff knew how to make good players into great ones. In my opinion, this is what all coaches must strive to do. However, most coaches do not understand how to train players to be great. They focus too much on the mechanics of the game. While mechanics are important to a player's development, once an individual attains a certain proficiency, what's next? This is the point where coaches must break away from mainstream instruction.

Playing for Coach Cheff, I learned that attitude, confidence, mental toughness, and work ethic are the qualities that distinguish truly great players from merely good ones. All of these qualities were forged into me during my time at L-C State. Today, I try to instill them into athletes of all ages who have the desire to play at a high level. In conjunction with proper mechanics, the right mindset will give players an opportunity to maximize their full potential.

The Mindset of the Hitter

I learned many things in my two years at L-C State, but the most important is the role of the hitter's mindset. I hardly ever hear coaches talk with their hitters about mentality, plan, and approach. Most are too caught up in swing mechanics. Yet these very things greatly affect the development of the hitter.

Mechanics do not make great hitters, mentality does. Without the proper mindset, hitters will struggle even when their swing mechanics are good. I see this all the time—cage All-Americans, 5 o'clock hitters, and BP hall of famers with pretty swings who can mash in the cage but can't produce in the game. Usually, the reason is something mental. I've seen cases where the opposite is true: good hitters who have small flaws in their swings but who are never exposed because they have the right mindset.

Once a player can routinely duplicate his swing correctly, he is ready to develop the mindset necessary for him to have a chance to become great. Players and coaches need to understand that there is much more to hitting than what they are usually taught. The hitter's mentality, plan, and approach are the keys to real on-field improvements.

Mentality

Along with good vision and pitch recognition, the hitter's mental approach greatly influences his chance to succeed. Through my experiences with players and coaches, I have learned that the mental part of hitting instruction is almost non-existent. When I ask most coaches what they are teaching their players regarding hitting, the answer is almost always something mechanical. The funny thing is, most mechanical problems relate directly to a poor mental approach. It is our job as coaches to emphasize the mental aspects of hitting just as much as the mechanics. Most of the ideas in this section are appropriate for all ages, but use good judgment depending on the abilities of each player.

Be in the box ready to hit: *All* hitters must get in the batter's box with the mindset of being ready to hit. Being "ready to hit" doesn't mean the hitter should step up and try to see the ball and hit the ball. This approach will give hitters the wrong idea about what their mindset should be. As I stated in Chapter 3, no hitter, especially at the higher levels, has enough time to recognize the pitch, decide whether to swing, and then react. Instead, hitters must focus on a "yes" mentality. With the "yes" mentality, the hitter is expecting the pitch to be a strike. By thinking "yes," he is prepared to swing at every pitch until the ball says "no." The hitter must be ready crush every pitch, thinking, *yes, yes, yes, YES!* (swing) if the pitch is a strike, or, *yes, yes, yes, NO!* (don't swing) at the last moment if the pitch is a ball. If any part of the hitter's thought process says "maybe," he's setting himself up for failure before the pitch is even thrown. There should be no "maybe" in the mind of the hitter. To compete against good pitching, the hitter has to be 100% sold-out to a "yes" mentality.

Andrew Moore

Be fastball-ready: Great hitters always anticipate a fastball and then adjust if they recognize an off-speed pitch. They don't look for off-speed because they don't want to be late if they see fastball. You have to take pride in not missing fastballs, especially when a pitcher misses his spot. By "not missing," I mean the hitter needs to put the ball in play *hard*. Make the pitcher pay the price for leaving a fastball out over the plate. It may be the only good pitch the hitter sees in that at-bat.

For most hitters, fastballs located on the black/down and away are very hard to hit. Unless a player likes that pitch, I generally encourage hitters to take it early in the count. Other than the pitch low and away, hitters simply must consistently make solid contact on fastballs. To sum it up, don't miss the fastball, and definitely don't take fastballs that should be crushed.

Be selective: A hitter with good pitch selection is able to hit the strikes and lay off the balls. Great hitters have this ability, and they rarely chase bad pitches out of the strike zone. They force the pitcher into more hitter's counts, and to throw fastballs for strikes. More fastballs equals more success, especially when the hitter knows it's coming.

Competition and the Aggressive Mindset

I see hitters who can't get the job done because they are just too timid, or too concerned with how their swing looks. Hitting is not a fashion show, it's a battle. Hitters must go into *every* at-bat with controlled aggression and the mindset that nothing the pitcher can do will get them out.

Mental toughness starts with an aggressive, competitive attitude at the plate. Today, a lot of hitters lack an aggressive approach to hitting because coaches focus too much on mechanical principles. An aggressive mentally will enable the hitter to explosively react—and to gain an edge over his competition.

At L-C State, Coach Cheff had a unique and notorious way of creating competition among players: the boxing smoker. Prior to the season, each of us would be matched up with a teammate to fight for three rounds in a real boxing ring. No one knew his opponent until the day of the event, so the anticipation was incredible. On fight day, each of us was introduced by our boxing nickname with intro music like "Eye of the Tiger" playing in the background. The other players would gather around the ring to watch the match, most of them reluctantly awaiting their own fights.

Players would leave with broken noses, black eyes, swollen faces, and other minor injuries, but also definitely a feeling of relief and accomplishment. Coach Cheff used the boxing smoker to build mental and physical toughness among his players, but more importantly to help them overcome fear and anxiety. Guys feared getting in the ring and boxing without a lot of training or experience. But after the boxing smoker, playing in a national championship game seemed easy.

I don't use this example to say that coaches should buy two pairs of boxing gloves and make their players duke it out. However, it does show how a fearless and aggressive mindset can make a player mentally tough. An aggressive mentality helps tremendously in improving a player's confidence at the plate. A hitter's confidence is built through success on the field, and success is earned through hard work, determination, and a level of commitment that tests and builds the hitter's mental toughness.

Once hitters have success at the plate, confidence will drastically increase. A confident hitter is a dangerous hitter, and watch out when this confidence is finally earned. Be careful not to let this confidence turn into cockiness. No one enjoys a cocky player. With hitting, if a player gets too cocky, I promise you that he will get humbled sooner or later. Let the attitude be tough and aggressive, and let the confidence be quiet.

This next concept may sound a little crazy but it's part of an aggressive mindset and I believe in it wholeheartedly. It is the idea of training hitters not to move out of the way of a pitch that is thrown at them.

Getting hit by a pitch helps in two ways. First, it trains hitters to be mentally and physically tough. Second, when a pitcher hits the batter, it gives the team a base runner and base runners produce runs. The only thing that must be learned is how to get hit correctly. The idea is to turn the front shoulder in, toward the catcher, and to try to wear the pitch somewhere on the backside of the body. Other than that, there is no exact science to it, just a mindset of toughness. Hitters must realize that being hit by the pitch is part of the game and is totally out of their control. No one wants to get hit by a pitch but there is no getting around it and sometimes it definitely hurts.

I remember the first time I was introduced to this concept at L-C State. I had to learn the hard way that the batter's box is my area and I'm not moving! We were playing an inter-squad game and a freshman jumped back out of the way of an inside pitch. Coach Cheff calmly stopped the game, went to the cages, and got out the pitching machine. We thought we were going to hit off of the machine, live on the field. Little did we know that Coach Cheff had something else on his mind that would teach us a serious lesson about a hitter's mentality.

He put the machine on the mound, set the speed at about 90 mph, and lined it up right at the hitter. Each of us had to stand in there and get hit three times. Having 90-plus-mph fastballs shot at me was one of the scariest things I ever had to do, but I learned a lesson about the mental and physical toughness necessary to compete at that level, and was reminded how being hit by the pitch can help the team. That year, we won a national championship and as a team were hit by pitches almost 150 times.

I'm not advocating that we teach Little Leaguers to stand in there and be tough, never moving out of the way of a pitch. But, probably starting around high school, players should learn how getting hit by a pitch can help create a tough and aggressive mindset. It can also affect the outcome of the game. So take pride in not moving (unless the pitch is going right at your head)!

What separates the good hitters from the great hitters is the mentality they bring to the plate. Developing a mindset that is aggressive, tough, confident, and ready to hit are all important elements in becoming a great hitter. If someone has the desire to play at a high level, mental maturity is mandatory. The next step is understanding "plan and approach." This requires players to study the pitcher and to focus on what they have to do to be successful in each individual at-bat. The mental approach will often dictate whether or not the hitter has consistent, successful results on the field.

Finally, hitters must learn how to deal with the ups and downs involved with hitting. Nobody gets a hit every time, and everyone will strike out. It's part of the game. How the hitter deals with failure is what matters most. The ability to learn from the last at-bat and quickly move on is key to dealing with adversity. Hitters are only as good as their last at-bat, and are always only one swing away from a hitting streak.

When a hitter struggles with confidence, other problems related to mentality can surface. Putting too much pressure on the situation, thinking too much, and being afraid to fail are all mental components that can hinder the hitter's ability to create consistent quality at-bats.

The Hitter's Plan

Plan and approach is another huge aspect of the hitting mentality. If the hitter is not prepared to compete before he steps into the box, or he does not have a plan, he's far less likely to be successful.

In my opinion, teaching the mental plan and approach to hitting is one of the hardest things to do. This is because coaches must reinforce the mental aspects of hitting without causing the hitter to over-think his at-bats. On one side of the dilemma, hitters have to think about their approach in every at-bat. On the other side, if a hitter gets into the habit of thinking too much and does not let his natural ability lead the way, he'll be a mental mess at the plate.

Before the game: Different aspects of the plan and approach to hitting depend greatly on the level of competition. The approach of a big-leaguer is going to be detailed and complex. He can incorporate advanced scouting reports on pitcher's tendencies, video technology, and the advice of coaches and players around him. High school and college players may have some scouting reports, but generally their information is limited to what is seen on the field. Younger players must simply rely on their coaches to teach the basic concepts of the mental approach. Regardless, no matter the level of play, every hitter must learn from his mistakes and make adjustments.

Hitters should start thinking about their game approach when they see the opposing pitcher warming up in the bullpen. Watching the pitcher before the game, in between innings, and during other hitters' at-bats is one area of the game where hitters must pay attention. During these times, critical information about the pitcher's tendencies and weaknesses can be recognized. You learn many things about a pitcher just by watching them warm up: How hard does he throw? Is he throwing strikes? What off-speed pitches does he throw? Where is his release point? Is he missing low or high?

During the game: Even more information about the pitcher can be determined by analyzing other players' at-bats. Does the pitcher throw a lot of first-pitch fastballs? Does the fastball have movement? Does he like to pitch inside or outside? Does he throw off-speed for strikes? Does the pitcher tip off any of his pitches? I could go on but I think you get the point.

While this information will help hitters in their plan and approach, the only way to gather it is to pay attention. Hitters sometimes have no clue when they step to the plate because they never watch the game. Studying each individual pitcher will provide valuable information that will prepare hitters to enter the batter's box with a plan.

Jake Stein

The coaches and players in the dugout should figure out most of the information about the plan and approach. It should then be taken by each hitter into the on-deck circle. On-deck preparation is an important aspect in getting ready to hit. Many hitters don't get ready early enough. They are often times rushed on deck, trying to quickly put on their helmet and batting gloves. This tardiness does not allow enough time to prepare physically or mentally. All hitters should eagerly anticipate their at-bat and be ready to go by the time they are in the hole (even with two outs). The time spent on deck should be used to get loose, time the pitcher, and mentally focus. Hitters should find a consistent routine that allows them to prepare for each and every at-bat. I like to see hitters take at least two aggressive hacks to get loose, while timing the pitcher on every pitch. If there is time, the hitter can think of little mechanical reminders, however, they should NEVER think about mechanics at the plate. One of the most important things that hitters need to do on deck is to mentally focus on their plan and approach. A hitter with a plan is mentally prepared to hit.

The Hitter's Approach

A hitter's mental plan and approach to each at-bat depends on the pitching. Hitters cannot take the same approach with every pitcher. They *must* adjust. I've heard a lot of bad excuses throughout my years of teaching hitting, but the best ones are when players say things like, "He pitches too slow. I can't hit slow pitching." Or, "That pitch was too low."

The pitcher is not there to give the hitter what he wants. I like to joke with hitters who make these kinds of excuses that next time they get into the batter's box, they should call timeout (I usually tell them to use one of their 30-second timeouts) and politely communicate the speed and location they would like so they can hit

Alec Dingle

it. They quickly get the point that adjustments need to be made. Pitchers have the same mindset of battling on every pitch, doing everything in their power to get the hitter out.

The overall concept in creating the proper approach is pretty simple: don't do what the pitcher is trying to make you do. It sounds easy enough but trying to get it done in a game is another thing that makes hitting so hard. Hitting would be easy if pitchers threw the same pitch at the same velocity every time (no matter how hard they throw). Unfortunately, pitchers do not do this. Pitchers will try to do different things to get hitters out depending on what they do best. Some throw slower and try to get hitters out front, while others try to overpower hitters with velocity. Some throw a lot of junk and rely on movement; some throw a lot of fastballs and rely on location. Some throw a lot of strikes and pitch to contact; others try to make hitters fish for pitches just outside of the strike zone. Whatever the case, for a hitter to be successful, he must be able to quickly adapt and adjust his approach to each pitcher.

Soft-tossers: A pitcher who throws slowly wants to get the hitter swinging too far out in front. To not let that happen, the hitter's approach should be to move as far up in the box as possible and to get closer to the plate. Slow pitchers cannot beat good hitters with anything inside and normally live on the outer part of the plate. Scooting up on the plate takes away their bread and butter, while moving up in the box helps in not getting too far out in front.

Andreas Plackis

Justin Folz

Nick Tieskoetter

The mental approach should be to let the ball travel and to think about driving the ball middle away. By thinking middle away they will still hit it hard to their pull side if they end up a little out front (but not on purpose). Hitters who do not take the proper approach end up getting themselves out by rolling over, hitting the ball off of the end of the bat, or getting too far out front and hitting weak pop ups.

Power pitchers: Hitters must take a totally different approach to a pitcher who throws hard. Most pitchers who throw hard will challenge hitters with a lot of fastballs. A fastball-ready mentality is essential. The hitter should load little earlier than normal, with his hips and hands ready to fire right after the ball is released. He must focus on early pitch recognition, and speeding his eyes up to see the ball quicker. The plan should be to get the hands out in front of the body at contact so if he is late to the pitch, he will still have a chance to drive the ball the opposite direction. The hitter should focus on trying to hit the top half of the ball. I don't think I have ever watched a college or big-league game and seen a hitter foul a ball into the dirt over the top of a hard, straight fastball. It just doesn't happen, unless it is a fastball with some sink to it. Quite often, what we do see is hitters being consistently late and underneath the hard fastball. The adjustment should be to hit the top half out front. Whenever there is a hard thrower, the mental approach should always be about being quick to the ball. The velocity of the pitch will provide the power, so all the hitter has to do is make square, solid contact and the ball will fly. By keeping an aggressive, but quick, fastball-ready mindset, the hitter has a better opportunity to square up a ball from a pitcher that throws gas. And remember to not miss the fastball.

Junk-throwers. Another type of pitcher where hitters need to take a different approach is one who throws a lot of junk. These pitchers throw a lot of off-speed pitches and are not afraid to throw them in any count. They will often pitch backward, throwing off-speed pitches in fastball counts and fastballs in off-speed counts. Junk pitchers rely on getting hitters to swing at a lot of balls just outside of the strike zone and get them to take a lot of strikes. If this type of pitcher has any velocity whatsoever, he will be very hard to hit. Hitters will often overthink facing this type of pitcher and guess incorrectly at the pitches that are being thrown. The mentality that a hitter needs to take to the plate against a junk pitcher should be patient and selectively aggressive. The main goal is letting the ball travel and driving the ball the opposite way. Hitters should still be loaded ready to hit (and not miss) the fastball and must be able to capitalize on any mistakes. To be successful hitting the pitcher's mistakes, there has to be adjustments made to the movements of the different pitches. The hitter must also patiently work the count, only swinging at strikes. He should never be scared to hit with two strikes because hitters will normally get a least one good pitch to hit per at-bat. Make sure to expect a good pitch and don't miss it when it finally comes. Hitting against a pitcher that throws a lot of junk can get frustrating at times, especially with the wrong approach. Going to the plate with the right plan will help the hitter avoid doing what junk pitchers want him to do. Be patient, do not miss the pitches that should be crushed, and battle hard without over thinking.

Left-handers and sidearmers. I am not going to spend a lot of time on the approach for lefties and sidearmers because they will fall into one of the previous categories. However, I will give a couple tips that will enable a hitter to adjust properly. For left-handed pitchers and sidearmers, the biggest adjustments are where to focus the eyes and hitting the different moving pitches. Both of these pitchers throw from different release points so hitters have to adjust their vision according to where the pitch is being released. Since different release points cause various pitch movements, hitters have to adjust to what they see. This can only be done by repetitively hitting all types of pitches from different angles so that the muscle memory will eventually make hitting different pitches more natural.

One of the best ways that I learned how to develop this muscle memory was when I was in college. At the time, there were about four outdoor cages where we would hit in practice. Each cage had a machine set up that threw a different pitch. For example, one cage could be set up for a hard right-handed fastball and the next maybe a right-handed slider. Another cage could have a left-handed fastball away, and in the last cage something like a slow left-handed curveball. Every day, the machines were set up differently to throw about every pitch imaginable. We would rotate through each cage hitting all of the different pitches, forcing us to make quick adjustments.

I remember the first time I attempted to hit off of these machines. I hated it because I had no chance. The machines were hard to time and I had never really worked on hitting pitches that moved that much, especially at that velocity. I was used to the typical live-arm batting practice pitches that had little movement or speed, so I was never actually pushed to improve. Hitting off the machines was a humbling experience but over time I got used to hitting every possible pitch. Looking back, the repetition of hitting off of each machine every day honed my ability to hit all different pitches and also made the in-game pitches look easier to hit. By seeing various game-like pitches coming from different angles on a regular basis, I learned how to adjust to the different pitchers. I highly recommend that more advanced hitters spend time hitting off of machines that can throw different pitches. Even though machines are often hard to time, they give a real game-like effect of what the ball will be doing out of a pitcher's hand. It also forces hitters to figure out how to adjust their timing. Each and every pitcher is different, so it is very important that hitters train themselves to adjust their approach from pitcher to pitcher.

Making Adjustments

Before making adjustments to the pitcher, hitters must know their own personal strengths and weaknesses and always hit to their strengths. A good example of this would be if a hitter crushes inside pitches but struggles on hitting pitches away, he should move up closer to the plate. Moving closer to the plate allows him to hit to his strength because it makes the outside pitch closer to him while still feeling comfortable because of his ability to consistently handle pitches inside. Hitters should always know what they do best, where they struggle, and adjust accordingly.

Hitters must make little adjustments during the game, and even during at-bats. A player might go into an at-bat with a specific plan of letting the ball travel because the pitcher did not appear to be lighting up the radar gun in his warm ups. After seeing the first fastball blow by, the hitter had better quickly adjust his approach and timing to get his hands out front.

If a hitter is consistently late or early to the ball, the adjustment can be pretty simple. The first thing that I always ask hitters when I begin working with them is where they usually hit the ball. This will typically give a good idea of the mental adjustments that need to be made to help fix their individual problem. If they are always late and hit every ball to the opposite field, the adjustment should be to get their hands out front at contact and try to pull the pitch. If they are always early to the pitch and pull everything, they need to let the ball travel and drive the ball to the opposite field. These adjustments sound elementary but are mandatory to start with when making in-game adjustments or fixing consistent problems. The idea here is to show hitters that they must learn to make little mental adjustments during their at-bats.

Other little adjustments can be as simple as trying to hit a different part of the ball. Believe it or not, it is possible to take a perfect swing and miss-hit the ball on the top or bottom half. For someone who is popping up a lot, or fouling balls off under the ball, the adjustment and approach could be as easy as trying to hit the top half of the ball (and vice versa for someone who hits a lot of ground balls). Making minor adjustments on the contact point of the ball should be the first thing that hitters with good mechanics focus on when they are

Troy LaBrie

struggling at the plate. Most of the time when hitters slump, they try and fix things mechanically, end up thinking too much, and making things worse. However, often the hitter can address the results on the field by simply focusing on hitting slightly higher or lower on the ball. Hitters should start with small mental adjustments before jumping into mechanical repairs (unless there is something major going on).

As you can tell, adjustments are very important in hitting. The plan and approach to hitting even focuses on the umpire and their individual strike zone. It is important to know how wide the strike zone gets, if the zone is big or small, or if high or low strikes are being called. Because of where they set up, most umpires will have a wider zone on the outside part of the plate but will be pretty consistent on the inside strike call.

If hitters pay attention to what is being called for strikes and what is not, they can adjust their mental approach. For example, if the umpire has a smaller strike zone, the hitter can be more selective looking for better pitches to hit. On the contrary, if the strike zone is big, they better not be too picky in their pitch selection and have a more aggressive approach to hittable pitches. Some umpires are so inconsistent with their strike zones that hitters must do everything in their power to battle and compete. No matter how good or bad the umpire, the strike zone is something hitters cannot control. When (not if) there are bad strike calls, *get over it!* I see too many hitters get mad or frustrated on bad calls and let their emotions affect the rest of their at-bat. When this happens, the hitter must have the attitude of, "So what! I didn't want to hit that pitch anyway," and then focus on the next pitch. If there are two strikes and the umpire calls a borderline pitch a strike, it's the hitter's fault for allowing the umpire to decide his fate for him. Hitters must be able to quickly forget and move on if the call does not go their way. Great hitters do not let one questionable call affect the outcome at the plate!

A.J. Schramm

Bottom of the 4th

After the foundation of an explosive, mechanically sound swing is established, hitters must continually focus on understanding and improving their mental approach. The mental aspects that allow hitters to compete on a higher level take an enormous amount of time to learn. To fulfill their potential, hitters must be mentally tough with a controlled, aggressive mindset. An attitude of confidence and trust in their ability only comes with success on the field. Opportunities for success are created when hitters step into the box ready to hit, with a "yes" mentality that anticipates a fastball and is aggressively selective only to pitches in the strike zone.

Hitters must study each pitcher and his tendencies in order to plan for the proper approach during each at-bat. Adjustments must always be made to the various types of pitchers if hitters want to have consistent, quality at-bats. There is much more involved with the mentality of hitting in the next chapter. The ideas covered in this chapter are the foundation.

Coaches and hitters need to realize that hitting is more about the mentality than mechanics. Mechanics are important, but a hitter will never understand how to hit unless he learns the mental concepts that will help him compete on every pitch. Great hitters compete with passion and intense focus. The brutally honest truth is that hitters who do not develop a hitter's mentality have no chance to competing at a high level. The hitter's mentality dictates the hitter's future!

End of the Inning

Mechanics do not make players great, the mentality does!
Hitting is not a fashion show, it's a battle!

Chapter 4

5th Inning
Developing the Ultimate Hitter

Vision, pitch recognition, and maximizing your full potential

Great hitters have more than just a great swing. They have the instincts, intelligence, and awareness necessary to take their hitting to a higher level. They become "baseball smart" by studying the way the game is supposed to be played. They understand the little things, like situational hitting, drag bunting, and hitting in different counts. These hitters have learned (sometimes having taught themselves) the essential requirements for *real* hitting. Because of their intellect, they can do things average hitters cannot.

Before a hitter can learn how to hit specific pitches, hit in different counts, or hit situationally, he must realize the importance of vision and pitch recognition. Without them, he cannot hit! This is a harsh statement, but it is one of the greatest truths in all of hitting.

Over the years I have used two approaches to help hitters see the pitch better: speeding up the eyes, and seeing the ball into the box.

"Speeding up the eyes" means seeing the ball quicker out of the pitcher's hand, allowing the hitter to recognize pitches earlier and see the ball longer. "Seeing the ball into the box" is about understanding the strike zone and where to focus the eyes. Imagine the strike zone as an invisible box. The hitter's vision focuses simultaneously on the pitcher's release point for pitch recognition as well as the box at the plate. This invisible box will expand or shrink depending on the count, situation, umpire's strike zones, and the hitter's individual strengths and weaknesses. Hitters must make consistent, quality contact with the pitch in the box, but this will only happen if there is early pitch recognition.

A hitter can dramatically improve vision and pitch recognition through game-like repetition in practice and live game at-bats. The problem today is that many coaches become so consumed with swing-functions that they hardly ever work on improving a hitter's pitch recognition.

When a hitter has learned how to consistently control the foundational movements of their swing, he is ready to learn how to hit specific pitches in all areas of the strike zone. They are also ready for the basic mental approach to hitting with different counts. Situational hitting can be introduced as well, but it will become more important as the athlete plays at the high school, college and professional levels. Bunting should be taught at a young age regardless of swing mechanics and is a huge part of the game especially for players with good speed.

The challenge is that the concepts in this chapter can take years to develop, and for the more serious hitter it is a never-ending process. Developing the ultimate hitter is not something that happens overnight. It takes time, hard work, extreme dedication, and a lot of God-given ability. There are many things to learn, so be patient in the process.

Hitting Inside vs. Outside Pitches

These two pitch locations create slight differences in the mechanics of the swing that all hitters must learn. In other words, hitting inside vs. outside pitches requires the hitter to have two different swings to the ball. Although they are minor differences, it is important for the hitter to understand their swing mechanics should not be exactly the same when trying to hit balls on opposite sides of the plate. The swings will differ in four ways: the hitter's posture; contact point of the pitch; what the hips do; and the hand path to ball.

Posture: The hitter's posture will be slightly different on an inside pitch compared to an outside pitch. For successful contact to occur on an inside pitch, the hitter must stay more stacked or upright with little to no body weight movement created in toward the plate. A "falling in" movement toward the plate will almost always cause the hitter to get tied up on an inside pitch. However, hitting an outside pitch should create a little postural momentum leaning over the plate that will help the hitter reach the pitch and stay through it more easily. Staying stacked on an inside pitch and a little lean on pitches away greatly increases the hitter's chances to arrive on time and on plane.

Contact point: The desired contact points on both the inside and outside pitches are very easy to explain and understand. However, it's not easy for the hitter to get the barrel head to these contact points when he has no idea where the pitch is going to be located.

Contact on inside pitches must be out front somewhere close to the hitter's stride foot, while the outside pitch must travel farther and contact should be made somewhere between the front knee and the middle of the body (still on the front side of the body). These contact points vary slightly depending on how far in or out the pitch is and how well the hitter recognizes the pitch. No matter what type of pitch is thrown (fastball, changeup, curveball, etc.), inside pitches are contacted out front while outside pitches are contacted a little deeper. Sounds simple, but this is one of the things that make hitting so hard.

Failure to make contact in these ideal areas will cause unwanted results. If the inside pitch gets too deep, a "jam sandwich" is inevitable. If the inside pitch is contacted too far out front, common occurrences are to roll over or to pop up weakly, and it is very hard to keep the ball in fair territory. Outside pitches that travel too deep will be consistently fouled off or popped up, and outside pitches that are contacted too far out front will usually get rolled over or hit off of the end of the bat. Hitters who cannot consistently make solid contact in the correct hitting zones have holes in their swings that will get picked apart by good pitching.

What the hips do: Hitting inside pitches successfully is all about quick hip rotation. When the hitter recognizes an inside pitch, his hips must quickly, fully rotate. The hips on an outside pitch should never fully rotate (but should still be explosive); they should only get about one-half to three-fourths of the way through. This enables the hitter to let the ball travel deeper and get better extension through the ball. If the hips fully rotate on the outside pitch, the tendency will be to pull the hands off the ball, which leads to rolled over ground balls. If the hips don't fully rotate on the inside pitch, most of the time the hands will drag to the ball and the pitch will be contacted too deep. If hitters understand the difference in how the hips work on inside vs. outside pitches, it makes hitting pitches on both sides of the plate a lot easier.

Hand path: The hand path to the ball has the most important role in hitting pitches in and out. I see a lot of hitters who throw their hands to the same spot on every pitch and then try to adjust mid-swing to the pitch location. It just does not work. Hitters must learn to take their hand path to the location of the pitch. The hand path is always going to be moving forward to the pitch but it is forward moving away from their body on the outside pitch, or forward staying close to their body on a pitch inside. Hitters who cannot execute the proper hand paths to varying pitch locations will only make successful contact on pitches that are thrown into their unchanging swing pattern. In other words, unless the pitch is thrown into their wheelhouse, they cannot hit. Great hitters must be able to recognize pitch location and then move their hands accordingly.

A hitter has to be able to control both sides of the plate. He must be quick enough to be able to get to an inside pitch and let the ball travel deep enough to hit the outside pitch. This is a hard thing to do and is only accomplished with repetition and good pitch recognition. When hitters improve their ability to control both sides of the plate, they give themselves a better opportunity for successful contact.

Jordan Siu

Understanding what needs to take place to successfully square up both inside and outside pitches is one thing. Being able to consistently accomplish this task is a whole different ball game. Mastering the ability to hit inside and outside pitches is hard because the strike zone is usually wider than the actual plate itself. Umpires consistently call strikes one or two ball-widths off the plate (at *all* levels), so hitters should practice hitting pitches a little off of the plate in and out. If umpires only called strikes on pitches that were on the plate, hitting inside and outside pitches would be a lot easier, but they don't, so players must train themselves to handle pitches slightly off the plate.

All great hitters possess awesome plate coverage. If the hitter spends quality time working on the correct contact points, hip rotation, and hand paths of inside vs. outside pitches, his on-field performance will improve dramatically.

Hitting High vs. Low Pitches

A big part of developing the ultimate hitter is to train him to lay off the shoulder-high fastball and to learn what it takes to hit the pitch low in the zone. Pitchers are taught to work low in the zone because hitting a low pitch is harder than hitting a waist-high pitch, and the consequences of missing a spot low in the zone are not as severe. Not only is the low pitch harder to hit, most umpires will call the pitch slightly below the knees a strike. You have no idea how many times I see hitters whining and complaining when the pitch barely below their knees gets called a strike. I try to explain that the *real* strike zone is not from the waist to the knees, but from the waist to below the knees. Hitters must submit and realize that the umpire's strike zone is something they cannot control and that umpires are not going to stop calling this pitch a strike any time soon. Since this is prevalent at all levels, teaching hitters how to hit the low pitch is mandatory but often overlooked.

To achieve successful contact on a low pitch, two things must occur. The hitter's backside has to stay low (bent) and his eyes must stay down with the pitch. This is why the lower half of the body plays such a crucial role in swing mechanics. If the back leg does not stay down, and it has the tendency to jump up or out, the hitter has no chance for successful contact. Hitters who jump out of their backside will not square up pitches located low in the zone, and if they do, they usually chop it into the ground. I use the term "stay in your legs" more than you could imagine. This means that no matter what pitch is thrown or where it is thrown, the backside must stay bent, especially on low pitches. However, a bent backside does not mean that the back knee sinks down towards the ground. The difference between a sinking backside and a bent backside is when the backside sinks, the front knee bends as well, which makes the hitter's eyes sink with it. A bent backside means the back knee drives forward and down towards the front toe, but the eyes stay level because there is no sinking motion in the legs.

Don't get me wrong, there are times when swinging at a really low pitch out of the strike zone forces the hitter to sink in their legs in order to make contact with the ball. This is something that all hitters must do if they are fooled by the pitch and commit to swinging at it. But if a hitter can consistently stay balanced and level in their backside without sinking, he will be less likely to swing at pitches that are low and out of the zone.

The eyes also factor into the hitter's ability to handle the low pitch. Think of the eyes and the backside as being connected. If the backside jumps up, the eyes will follow. If the backside stays bent, the eyes will stay down on the ball longer, which provides a better opportunity to hit a low pitch. The lower the pitch, the lower the eyes must go to get the barrel head behind the ball. The swing follows the eyes, so if the pitch is low, the eyes must stay low.

The main thing that hitters need to understand about a high pitch (mainly the high fastball) is that it is very hard to hit. I'm not talking about just above the waist; I'm talking about the shoulder-high fastball. A fastball at the top part of the strike zone is a great pitch to attack and should be hit hard every time. In fact, hitters are supposed to crush the waist-high pitch. However, a good fastball about chest high is a pitch that most hitters cannot handle. Great hitters will lay off it. If the hitter commits to swinging at a high pitch out of the strike zone, there is one major requirement: keep the hands above the ball. When the hands drop below the ball, the hitter is going to pop it up, foul it off, or swing and miss.

Some hitters can't lay off a high fastball. It looks so enticing because you can see it so well. I tell hitters two things to help them: 1) focus the eyes lower in the box (the strike zone), and 2) stay in their back leg. Keeping the backside bent helps tremendously with laying off of the high fastball. Weird! It seems like the backside-staying-bent thing is pretty important. When hitters jump out of their backside, the high pitch looks good. In fact, players who consistently jump out of their legs usually can hit high pitches and not much else. I suppose if the strike zone were from the waist to the shoulders, the backside would have to jump up to hit the ball, but it's not. So the goal should be to lay off the chest-high fastball, always crush the waist-high pitch, and practice hitting pitches that are low in the zone. The only way to make this happen is to keep the backside bent.

Hitting Off-Speed Pitches

The ability to hit off-speed pitches is important, but so is the ability to lay off them if they are not strikes. Hitters create positive outcomes when they can take curveballs and changeups that look like strikes out of the pitcher's hand but eventually move out of the strike zone. It makes pitchers have to throw strikes to get them out (they don't get themselves out by swinging at a bad pitch), it puts them in better hitter's counts, and forces the pitcher to throw more fastballs. When a hitter knows that a fastball is coming, it is easier to hit. It will also force the pitcher to adjust and throw these pitches on a good chunk of the plate. Great hitters have the ability to lay off curveballs and changeups off the plate, and mash the ones that pitchers leave over the plate.

Often, I hear coaches, parents, and players call out, "Watch for the curveball!" or "Watch for the changeup!" They think they're helping but they really are doing the hitter a disservice. Telling a hitter to watch for the off-speed pitch can shift his approach and cause him to be late on the fastball. A hitter should *never* look for an off-speed pitch because he won't catch up to the fastball. He should be fastball-ready and then adjust when he sees the off-speed pitch. Instead, maybe you should shout something like, "Look for the fastball and adjust." Better yet, if you're a parent, the only thing that you should really be shouting are encouraging words, not wrong instructions on how to hit.

The most popular principles shared by most coaches regarding hitting off-speed pitches are *keep the body weight back* and *let the ball travel into the hitting zone*. These are important, but there is more to hitting off-speed pitches than that. Hitters will not be able to stay back and let the ball travel if their swing is flawed. This is why the swing mechanics are so important. Swing mechanics are designed to enable hitters to hit pitches in all locations of the strike zone. Often, hitters do not understand why swing mechanics are what they are until they learn to hit off-speed pitches. Since most off-speed pitches will be down in the zone, all of the principles about hitting low pitches must be used. The most important things that will allow the hitter to stay back and let the ball travel are: staying down in their backside; keeping their eyes down; keeping their hands back; and getting big extension through the ball.

Curveballs: When he throws a curveball, the pitcher wants to get the hitter too far out front or to get him to ground out. To avoid this, hitters have to be able to let the ball travel but also to focus on hitting the bottom half of the ball. The swing path to a curveball should have a little more upward movement because the pitch is breaking down (remember, the goal is to get the barrel head on the same plane as the ball!). Curveballs breaking away require the hitter to use the principles described for hitting outside pitches: let the ball travel a little deeper and stay through it as long as possible. This does not mean hitters should always work on hitting the curveball that is breaking away down the opposite-field line. They should focus on driving this pitch hard up the middle or to the opposite field gap. And yes, it is OK to pull a curveball. There is nothing wrong with pulling a curveball that is left over the plate. In fact, that is what you are supposed to do when the pitcher makes a mistake. Make the pitcher pay.

A curveball that breaks toward a hitter is hit by using the principles for hitting an inside pitch. The hitter still has to let the ball travel, and focus on contacting the bottom half of the ball, but the main difference is that there must be an inside hand path to the ball. I tell hitters to hit the inside part of the ball on a pitch that is breaking in toward them. This will help get their hands inside the ball, to the proper contact point, and will give them a better opportunity to hit the ball in fair territory. The curveball that breaks into a hitter should be pulled or hit back up the middle depending on the location of the contact point. The back-door curveball is a very hard pitch to hit because it starts off the plate then breaks back over the outer corner. The advice I give to hitters is to let the ball come down, let it get deep, and then get big extension through the bottom half of the ball because the tendency is to roll it over.

Changeups: A good changeup is probably the hardest pitch to hit, because it looks like a fastball. Like the approach to hitting a curveball, the goal is to recognize it, let it travel deep, and stay back, but the reality is that the hitter is probably going to hit it way out front. I tell hitters they are probably going to lunge out a bit on a good changeup. It's normal (big-leaguers do it all of the time).

There are three things that must take place if lunging occurs: the eyes must stay down, focused on the bottom half of the ball; the hands must stay back; and the front side must stay closed. A closed front side is the

Luke Besel

front elbow staying down, not popping up, and the front shoulder not pulling out off the ball. This is not easy because the natural reaction to a fastball is to slightly lift the front elbow and slightly pull the front shoulder out as the hands are moving forward attacking the ball. Hitters who have a tendency to pull their front side out before they recognize the pitch usually struggle with hitting changeups.

Pitchers use off-speed pitches to try and fool hitters and get them off balance or too far out front. Even great hitters get caught lunging, but they still find a way to square up the pitch because they keep their hands back, eyes down, and stay through the pitch as long as possible (this is one of the reasons why extension is so important). In an ideal situation, the hitter will recognize the pitch, let the ball travel, and contact the ball in the correct contact area, but this is not going to happen all of the time. It is what the hitter does when he get fooled that gives them a chance for success.

With curveballs and changeups, coaches should encourage hitters to do two key things: speed up their swing through the contact point, and finish their swing aggressive—all the way over the shoulder with both hands staying on the bat. Hitters have to slow down their swing and flick their hands at the ball when they contact the ball too far out in front. By speeding up their swing at contact and finishing with both hands on the bat, the hitter will be forced to let the ball travel into the correct hitting zone. If the hitter cannot keep his top hand on the bat throughout the swing, use duct tape (I've done this and it works). Of the off-speed drills that I do, teaching hitters to speed up their swing with their top hand staying on the bat helps the most.

Learning how to consistently hit curveballs, changeups, and other off-speed pitches is no easy task and takes years of repetition. For success, the most important non-mechanical factor is pitch recognition. If you can't recognize a changeup, you won't hit it, no matter how sound your swing mechanics may be.

Josh Wilkes

Hitting With Different Counts

Knowing how to adjust his approach to the count is vital to the ultimate hitter's mentality. In my opinion, there are only three types of counts: offensive, very offensive, and extremely offensive. At no point should the hitter have a defensive mindset because it creates indecisiveness and uncertainty. The extremely offensive counts are 0-0 (first pitch), 2-0, 3-0, and 3-1. The very offensive counts are 0-1, 1-1, and 2-1. An offensive count is anything with two strikes. If you think about it, baseball and softball are the only games where you have the ball on defense. So hitters should always be offense-minded, even with unfavorable counts.

There are times when a hitter should take a first pitch, like when the team is losing late and needs baserunners, the hitter is undisciplined, or the pitcher can't throw a strike. Otherwise, I strongly disagree with coaches who do not allow hitters, especially young hitters, to be aggressive on the first pitch. Taking a first-pitch strike will put young hitters on the defensive and often lead to bad hitting counts. That first-pitch fastball might be the only good pitch the hitter will see during the at-bat.

It's upsetting (and comical) when I see coaches get angry when a hitter makes an out after telling them to take a first-pitch strike. Had they let the hitter swing away, the outcome may have been different. Instead, they put the hitter in a situation where he's forced into swinging at borderline pitches. Not all hitters are the same, but coaches should use caution when they make hitters take the first pitch.

It's also frustrating to watch a hitter stand there on his own and let a first-pitch fastball go by. To me, it shows that the hitter isn't ready to hit. What's worse is when the hitter rolls the next pitch over to the shortstop. He didn't make that out because of bad swing mechanics. His real problem was letting the previous pitch—his best chance at success—go right down the middle for a strike.

Extremely offensive counts: Whether the count is 3-1 or 2-0, the hitter's mindset should be exactly the same. He should be looking for a fastball in his favorite area, shrinking the invisible box (the strike zone). If he gets that pitch, he should crush it. If a pitcher does throw an off-speed pitch in one of these counts, the hitter should let it go. If the umpire calls it a strike, so what? You were sitting on a fastball anyway and the count is still in your favor. On these counts, I highly encourage hitters to start their swing a little earlier, anticipating the ideal fastball. Great hitters will never be late to the ball in these counts because they know a fastball is coming and they will be all over it.

Most of the time the hitter will take a pitch on a 3-0 count. If there is an opportunity to swing in this count the pitch had better be absolutely perfect and it better be crushed. Good hitters become better hitters by being selectively aggressive in extremely offensive counts.

Very offensive counts: The hitter's approach to 0-1, 1-1, and 2-1 counts should be slightly different from the extremely offensive counts. He should still be ready to hit a fastball, but he must widen his invisible box to the normal size of the strike zone. In these counts, hitters must have the ability to hit off-speed pitches that hang higher in the zone. I personally liked to lay off any off-speed pitch until I had two strikes (unless it was left out over the plate). It depends on each individual's ability to hit off-speed pitches as well as to hit with two strikes. It's OK to take borderline pitches in these counts because there is still one strike to work with.

Two-strike counts: The approach is simple: compete, battle, and compete some more! With two strikes, the hitter must take pride in putting the ball in play hard downhill. Good things can happen when the ball is in play. He should *never* strike out looking. When I say never, I mean the hitter must have the attitude that taking a called third strike is completely unacceptable. A hitter who puts up a lot of backward K's will face questions about his desire to compete, his mental toughness, and his ability to perform at a high level.

With two strikes, the hitter must make adjustments both mentally and physically. First, he should widen his invisible box by a couple of inches or more depending on the umpire's strike zone. A hitter should never give the umpire a chance to punch them out by taking a borderline pitch. Other adjustments that I recommend include widening the stance, moving closer to the plate, and shortening up the swing by slightly choking up on the bat.

A wider stance can give the hitter less movement, more balance, and train the eyes closer to the hitting zone so he can see the ball better. Moving closer to the plate can take away the outside strike several inches off the plate. Shortening up the swing allows the hitter to see the pitch a little longer for better pitch recognition. Choking up slightly on the bat gives the hitter more control of the bat and helps him be quicker to the ball. Of course, the most important thing for a hitter is to compete with confidence and fearlessness.

No matter the count or situation, hitting demands an offensive mindset. Having a specific plan for different counts will improve the hitter's mental approach at the plate. Understanding hitting in different counts is a small, but very important, element in becoming the ultimate hitter.

Situational Hitting

Situational hitting demands self-sacrifice, which is hard to do. I didn't care one bit about situational hitting until college, where I became more team-oriented and less selfish.

There are many different philosophies about situational hitting that are taught at the higher levels. I am only going to cover a few of these approaches because situations differ depending on the team's strengths and weaknesses and the coach's individual style. The goal here is not to argue what is right or wrong but to give hitters an idea of what they should be trying to accomplish in various situations.

Situational hitting is a learned trait that improves with the hitter's understanding of the game. A player will never be a good situational hitter unless he dedicates time to learning the intricacies of the game. Watching big-league or college games live or on TV is a good way to learn. Focus on the approach of the hitter depending on the situation, including: the score; the inning; the number of outs; the location of the baserunners; the hitter's position in the lineup; who is on deck; and so on. By observing, a hitter can learn a lot about the plan and approach of specific situations. If the game is on TV, listen to what the commentators are saying about what the hitter is trying to do (be careful, because a lot of television broadcasters have no idea about hitting).

The object of situational hitting is to produce runs. Every team at some point will need to win games by quality situational hitting. Some teams will have to do it more than others depending on what type of hitters they have. Teams with a lot of power can rely more on the three-run homerun while others will have to produce runs with base hits, bunting, and situational hitting. The fact is, every game will have situations where the hitter must understand how to advance a runner or score a teammate. Situational hitting means getting the job done at any cost, even if the batting average has to suffer.

I could write a whole chapter on what a hitter should know, but I am only going to cover a few basic approaches to specific situations:

With a runner on first and nobody out, the traditional idea is to move the runner to second into scoring position (this depends on the inning and score of the game). Some coaches will bunt the baserunner over while others may hit and run. My philosophy is for the hitter to be aggressive and look for a pitch up that he can drive into the gap. The last thing anyone wants is a double play. I would almost rather see the hitter strike out (and you already know how I feel about that). If a hit-and-run is given in this situation, I teach hitters not to try to hit behind the runner but to hit the ball where it is pitched. On a hit-and-run, the (right-handed) hitter should be looking to drive a pitch middle-away, but if it's inside, crush that sucker to the pull side.

With a runner on second and one or two outs, I want to drive the runner in. If there are no outs, a right-handed hitter should be looking for a pitch middle-away so he can hit something hard to the opposite field. A left-handed hitter should be looking for a pitch he can pull. A ground ball to the right side will move the runner over to third (or scores him if it gets through). A line-drive base hit will at least move the runner to third or possibly allow him to score, but a pop out is a wasted at-bat (unless it is deep enough for the runner to tag up and advance). No coach would ever get upset in this situation if a hitter were to get a hit to the left side of the field. However, if he were to roll one over to third and not advance the runner, most coaches would get fired up (I am one of them). A hitter who does this is either selfish or doesn't understand the game. With a runner on second base and nobody out, the hitter's job is to move that runner to third. Get it done.

With a runner on third base and less than two outs with the infield in, the hitter should always look for a pitch up in the zone that he can drive to the outfield. In this situation, the hitter wins either way if he can hit the ball on a line or deep in the air. An outfield fly ball will either be a sac fly, which doesn't count against the ol' batting average, or it will find some grass for a hit. If the infield is playing back, a simple ground ball to the shortstop, second baseman, or first baseman will score a run. This is the sacrificial part of situational hitting that helps teams score runs.

However, if the infielders are playing in, a ground ball will more than likely not score the run; the hitter needs to be aggressive and drive the ball. And popping the ball up is the same as not moving the runner over from second to third with nobody out. It's flat-out unacceptable.

Any time the bases are loaded or runners are on first and second with nobody out, the hitter should be looking for a pitch to drive into the outfield and he must not miss it. Again, a ground-ball double play or a strikeout will extinguish his team's morale.

Stefan Rohacek

Obviously there are many more situations during a game that demand a specific approach from a hitter, and the ones I've briefly covered are way more detailed and complex at the college and professional levels. If hitters understand what to do in these basic situations, they will be more apt to figure out other situations as well. The key to situational hitting is understanding the game, having a plan, looking for a specific pitch or pitch location to help accomplish the task, and sacrificing self for the betterment of the team.

While most at-bats do not demand situational hitting, every at-bat requires the hitter to have the proper plan and approach. Rest assured, the hitter does not always have to sacrifice at-bats and see his average plummet. However, the ultimate hitter can hit situationally and get hits at the same time.

Bunting

Because of ever-changing bat regulations that limit the exit speed of the ball coming off of the bat, some coaches will resort to bunting more often to score runs. Bunting is a big part of the game and hitters must take pride in working on it. When to bunt is decided by the coach but hitters need to study the game so they understand how each type of bunt can produce a competitive advantage given the situation.

I am not going to spend an exhaustive amount of time on bunting (after all, the book is about hitting), but I will cover what hitters should know about sacrifice bunts, drag bunts, and push bunts. There are many different philosophies about the mechanical aspects of bunting, when it should be used, and who should do it. I will explain the basic foundational techniques for each type of bunt, but more importantly, the overall mental principles that hitters must understand.

My philosophy about bunting is simple: drag bunt, drag bunt, drag bunt. Hitters need to master the art of drag bunting and be so good at it that they can do it in sacrifice situations. Of course, there are times when a player must sacrifice his at-bat and do whatever it takes to get the bunt down. But, in my opinion, too often the bunt is only a sacrifice because players do not spend enough time learning how to bunt for a hit. I do not like the idea of giving up an out to move a runner. If a player puts enough time and effort into being able to consistently get the drag bunt down, he will increase his batting average, put more pressure on the defense, and give his team a better opportunity for a big inning. I look at it this way: when a hitter can bunt for a hit instead of having to sacrifice, good things will happen. He either moves the runner with a hit or moves the runner with a sacrifice. Either way, it's a win for the hitter and the team. There is obviously a little more risk involved when drag bunting compared to sacrificing but this is why hitters must make it a priority to work on it so much that drag bunting becomes as easy as sacrifice bunting.

Nowadays, there are many different philosophies on how to teach bunting mechanics. You can watch a college game and see two teams have totally different techniques. I really don't care about the exact bunting mechanics as long as the hitter gets the job done. If a coach has a specific way that he wants his hitters to bunt, that's fine. Do it. The reality is that bunting should not be that difficult, no matter how it is done.

Sacrifice bunting: Sacrifice bunts tend to be called for in close game situations where the team desperately needs to produce a run. The foundational sacrifice bunting techniques that I teach are basic and widely used. Starting from the normal hitting stance, the hitter should square early by rotating the body so that his chest is facing the pitcher. The arms should be slightly bent with the bat out in front of the top half of the hitting zone. The legs should be bent and the hitter's eyes should be low and behind the barrel of the bat. The bat angle is controlled by the bottom hand and dictates what side of the field the ball will be bunted. The height adjustment to the pitch should be controlled by the hitter's legs moving up or down, never allowing the barrel of the bat to drop below parallel to the ground. The action of the actual bunt is to not to stab at the ball but to soften the contact point by slightly "giving" with the pitch. These essential principles will put the hitter in the best position to get the bunt down effectively. Sacrifice bunting is more detailed than this but hitter's need to take these basic principles and fuse them into whatever style their coach wants them to use.

Most sacrifice bunts are attempted by 1, 2, 8, and 9-hole-type hitters but at some point every hitter will be asked to get a bunt down. At the higher levels, all hitters work on getting the bunt down on the third base and first base sides so they will be ready when the team needs them. Understanding what side of the field to lay the sac bunt down is simple. Most coaches teach hitters to bunt the ball to the first base side with a runner on first and the third base side with a runner on second. I want to add that the hitter must adjust depending on what the defense is giving him. No matter where the ball is bunted, it must be bunted softly to advance the runner. If the runner advances, the hitter has done his job.

Drag bunting: A drag bunt is when a right-handed hitter tries to bunt for a hit down the third-base line. Any hitter with decent speed should make drag bunting a huge part of his game. Let's say a hitter has 200 at-bats in a year and gets an extra 10 hits by drag bunting. This could raise his average by about 50 points. Better yet, the threat of a drag bunt will make the corner infielders have to play in closer. This leaves bigger holes in the infield and increases the chance of a hit when the hitter swings away.

The four most important aspects to a successful drag bunt are reading the defense; showing it late; being quick out of the box; and placement of the ball. Bunting for a hit is easy when the hitter knows how to read the defense. Before the game, he should pay attention to the third baseman's athleticism and arm strength. A non-athletic third baseman or a third baseman with an average arm can mean an easy hit for a speedy drag bunter. Great drag bunters closely watch the positioning of the third baseman to see if he is playing even with, in front of, or behind the bag at third. A third baseman who plays behind the bag is giving the hitter a prime opportunity to beat out a bunt hit.

Field conditions play a role in analyzing opportunities to drag bunt. Before the game, the player should check out how fast or slow the infield plays, and whether the ball will want to funnel foul or stay fair. Field conditions can dictate where and how hard the hitter should bunt the ball. When hitters can analyze all of these things for themselves, they will have better knowledge and understanding of when to bunt for a hit. For a smart drag bunter, there is no bad time to bunt.

The element of surprise and getting out of the box quickly makes a huge difference. The later the hitter can show the drag bunt, the slower the third baseman will be to react. The extra step or two advantage is crucial to the hitter's chances to beat the ball to first.

Placement is often the most important aspect, even for hitters with average speed. The drag bunt should be located as close to the third-base line as possible. If the ball stays fair, it will almost always be a hit. If it goes foul, no harm is done and there is still a chance to hit. Bunting the ball back to the pitcher or not getting it close enough to the foul line is unacceptable and a waste of an at-bat.

The mechanics of a drag bunt are different from a sacrifice bunt. A right-handed hitter does not rotate his chest to face the pitcher as he would on a sacrifice; instead he must keep his chest facing first base. This puts the hitter in the best position to run as he bunts the ball. The hands quickly get the bat out in front, with the end of the bat pointing toward first base, creating the proper bat angle to bunt the ball to third. At the same time the hands are moving the bat out front, the hitter's back foot should take a small jab-step back behind his body. The front foot will quickly follow by taking a small step in the direction toward first base. Both feet should barely move before contact is made. The footwork enables the hitter to create the momentum needed for him to reach full speed out of the box within a couple steps. If done properly, there should be movement out of the box toward first even if the hitter takes the pitch.

For a left-handed batter, the difference is that the front foot must open up and take a small step toward first base while the back foot takes a small step to a position that's most optimal for running. The knob of the bat should point toward first base, creating the ideal bat angle to get the ball down the third-base line (a lefty drag bunt is down the third base line as well).

Push bunting: A push bunt uses the same principles as a drag bunt (reading the defense, showing it late, being quick out of the box, and placement of the ball). However, the placement and some of the mechanical functions are different. Correctly placed, a push bunt is extremely hard to defend.

Push bunts are done by right-handed hitters and hit down the first-base line. The goal is to bunt the ball hard enough to get by the pitcher into the area between the first and second basemen. If the ball gets past the pitcher and the second baseman fields it, there's a good chance that it will be a hit (if the fielders are playing normal depth). If the first baseman fields the ball, it should be an easy footrace to win between the hitter and the pitcher.

Footwork on a push bunt is exactly the same as a drag bunt from both the left and the right sides; the main difference is the bat angle and the hands. A push bunt is done by keeping the hands in close to the body with the knob of the bat pointing down the third-base line and extending the arms in a "pushing" motion at contact. The ball must be hit harder than a normal drag bunt but not so hard that it becomes an easy play for the first or second basemen. When a lefty bunts down the first base line, it is not really a push bunt; it is a drag bunt down the first-base side. The difference is that the bat angle must have the end of the bat pointing down the third-base line but all other principles and techniques are the same.

Bunting is a very important aspect of the game that most hitters do not spend a lot of time on. If a hitter has decent speed, he should make learning how to drag bunt a priority. I mean he should master it. Great hitters who can bunt for a hit bring a beneficial dynamic to not only their own game but also to their team as well. If you are a hitter who needs to add bunting to your game, start working on it now.

Bottom of the 5th

When I think of the ultimate hitter, I do not think of someone with a perfect swing. A great hitter will obviously possess exceptional bat speed, hand-eye coordination, vision, and pitch recognition. He can consistently contact the ball on time and on plane.

What really separates the great hitters from the competition is their ability to do things the average hitter cannot do. The ultimate hitter has the physical and mental prowess that allows him to hit inside and outside pitches; lay off high fastballs; hit pitches low in the zone; be on time when hitting off-speed pitches; apply the proper approach to different counts; hit for the betterment of the team (situational hitting); and bunt for a hit or sacrifice when needed. When a hitter can combine these things with the proper mentality, plan, and approach to hitting, he is on his way to developing into the ultimate hitter.

It is very rare to see a hitter who can consistently do all of these things, but a hitter who can execute all of these actions is pretty amazing to watch.

End of the Inning

If the hitter does not have good vision and pitch recognition, they cannot hit!
This is one of the greatest truths in all of hitting!

Jackson Brodman

Chapter 5

How to Use Slow Motion

Using slow-motion video to break down the swing

Several years ago, the dad of a player I'd been working with approached me with an open laptop in his hands. I could tell that he was fired up to show me something about his son's swing. Sure enough, he played me a slow-motion video of his son hitting off a tee in what looked to be a backyard somewhere.

I don't remember what the dad thought his son was doing wrong. What I do remember is watching slow-motion swings of someone whom I had already seen swing the bat tens of thousands of times in the cage and in games. In the video, the flaws I saw were not even close to what was really affecting this boy's swing. His real issue was that he was afraid of being hit by the pitch, which caused his front foot to step out and make everything pull off the ball. In this case, watching the hitter's swing in slow motion did nothing to help identify the cause of the problem.

I appreciated the dad's desire to help his kid, and quite honestly I am thankful that this incident happened because it gave me a better perspective on the advantages and disadvantages of using slow-motion video.

Live or Video?

If a hitter has really bad swing mechanics, analyzing swings on video is unnecessary because his problems are obvious. However, more advanced hitters will see their true weaknesses more clearly in slow motion.

Proper slow-motion video analysis starts with watching live game at-bats. Examining an advanced hitter's swing off a tee or during soft toss is a complete waste of time. What happens in a cage is not same as in a game. If there is no game footage, try to simulate a game situation with some kind of live pitch.

If the hitter does have game footage that can be broken down in slow motion, there are several things that must be identified before any analysis can begin. Many coaches will start picking apart a swing without ever recognizing important details that help determine the hitter's problem. This happens because most people think that all swing problems are mechanical and they immediately look for mechanical flaws. Remember from Chapter 2 that there is always a reason why mechanical things happen during the swing, and when analyzing a swing in slow motion, it is no different. Unfortunately, coaches are often too quick to jump to conclusions about what they see in slow motion. More than likely, what they see involves more than just mechanics.

See the Whole Picture

As a coach, you need to establish specific information in order to give the hitter the correct advice. Whether the pitcher is lefty or righty, the type of pitch, the velocity of the pitch, and the location of the pitch are all factors that may not be captured on video but will affect the swing you see. To use slow motion effectively, you need to look outside the frame and see the whole picture.

Let's say we're analyzing the swing of a hitter who is rolling over at contact. The video also shows that the hitter's head is pulling up slightly. If we were to stop there, we would see what is happening but not know why. We haven't gathered the information we need to give a quality assessment. We need to determine the outside influences that can affect the hitter.

With more information, we know that the hitter is swinging at a curveball low and away. Bad pitch recognition makes the hitter's head come up too early and he contacts the ball too far out in front. In this case, the root cause of rolling over on contact is the hitter not recognizing the curveball, and not necessarily rolling over or pulling his head up. Instead of focusing on keeping the head down longer and getting better extension through the ball, I would have him work on pitch-recognition drills and teach him how to hit a curveball.

One mistake coaches make when using slow-motion video is they overanalyze swing mechanics. It is possible for the swing to get too mechanical. This robotic swing is usually created when slow motion is used too much or gets too technical. These hitters may look good, but because of the overdose of slow-motion video analysis, their normal swing actually *becomes* slow motion!

With the focus always being on mechanics, coaches and hitters neglect to work on bat speed, timing, pitch recognition, and approach—the things that are necessary to becoming a better hitter. I recommend that coaches use video only once in a while, depending on the skill level of the hitter. If it is overused for the sole purpose of teaching mechanics, the tendency is for coaches to overanalyze and not allow the hitter's natural athleticism to come through at the plate. Remember, the purpose of using slow motion is to identify specific problems, not to manufacture swings that all look identical.

Big-League Swings

Analyzing a big-league hitter's swing in slow motion is a great way to show players the elements of a swing and how they come together. I think it should be mandatory for all athletes who are serious about playing baseball/softball in high school level or beyond to watch and learn how professionals swing the bat.

However, you should be careful when comparing younger hitters to big-leaguers.

The first problem is when a coach takes one specific slow-motion swing from a professional and uses it to clone all hitters. This is all over the Internet, especially on YouTube. A random coach will get way too mechanical about one swing, marking it all up with lines, circles, and arrows. He'll describe how the swing functions but *never* explain the outside influences that cause certain mechanical things to happen. The funny thing is you could put two slow-motion swings from the same hitter side by side and see two completely different swings depending on pitch recognition, pitch location, and the type of pitch.

Unfortunately, because they don't understand these outside influences, coaches will concoct ideas about hitting that are confusing or just not true. They'll show hitters one specific swing from a big-leaguer, which can give misleading information about how the swing should operate. The key point is to understand that just because a "coach" uses one swing of a big-leaguer to teach hitting, it doesn't mean that the hitter swings like that every time, or that all hitters should be compared to that specific individual.

Another thing to be careful with when comparing slow-motion swings of big-leaguers to younger hitters is the fact that not all hitters have the same problems or weaknesses. Making a young hitter copy the way a big-leaguer swings the bat won't fix his individual issues. Instead, watch his live game at-bats to identify the real problem. Then you can use slow motion to determine why this problem occurs.

Watching and comparing slow-motion swings of big-leaguers can help players see how the overall functions of the swing are supposed to work. If players only focus on duplicating the pros' mechanics, their swings may look better but they'll still have the same problems.

Also, big-league hitters are capable of things that coaches should not teach to younger hitters. A great example is to compare Albert Pujols to a 15-year-old high school kid who has a great swing but isn't very strong and doesn't have any power. Pujols is so strong and has such unbelievable bat speed that he doesn't need to load as big, transfer as much body weight, or take a stride when he swings. Instead of trying to duplicate the swing of a 6-foot 3-inch pro ballplayer, I would coach the 15-year-old to use his body weight more effectively to generate bat speed and power.

However, if this 15-year-old hitter were 6-foot-2 and 200 pounds, and serious in the weight room, he may benefit from some Pujols-like swing mechanics. It all depends on the individual's strengths and weaknesses. Do not take one swing of a big-leaguer and compare it to all hitters. Emulating someone who is not the same type of hitter will hinder a player's ability to maximize explosiveness and bat speed to the ball.

Misusing Slow-Motion Video

While slow-motion video can help a hitter recognize specific mechanical flaws, the biggest negatives arise from overanalyzing slow motion, misunderstanding what actually happens during a swing, and incorporating these misinterpretations into coaching.

I have worked with countless hitters who have been taught some of these misleading ideas. You know what? Most of them were not very successful because the stuff they were taught caused major swing flaws. It is upsetting to see hitters restricted because of invalid principles. I think that most of these false ideas are developed when slow motion is misused and misinterpreted. It happens all of the time. Coaches watch a swing in slow motion, inaccurately interpret the mechanical aspects, teach them incorrectly to hitters, and then cannot understand why their players are still having problems. The sad, brutal reality is that most coaches who try to teach hitting unknowingly are giving hitters wrong information about what swing mechanics are supposed to do. They are impeding, not helping, the hitter.

These misconceptions have been spread by people who spend *way* too much time analyzing big-league swings in slow motion. In doing so, they have concocted ideas about hitting that should not be thought about during the swing. A swing has to be quick. For slow motion to be beneficial, there must not be anything taught that compromises bat speed. These deceiving principles that are taught because of this misinterpretation of slow motion actually decrease the hitter's bat speed tremendously.

My intent is to tell the truth about what should not be taught in hitting, even when these mechanical things are easy to see in slow motion. Ultimately, the real causes of the improper use of slow motion originate from how things are explained to the hitter. To clarify, I will dissect the five most commonly taught misconceptions that arise from overanalysis of slow-motion video. They are: slotting the back elbow; starting the hips before hands; a locked front arm; lagging the bat; and an improper swing path to the ball. Let's look at each one.

Elbow Slot

Teaching hitters to slot their back elbow seems to be the new fad. The elbow slot occurs when the hitter's back elbow drops in toward his rib area to start the swing. Since this is something you see when watching big-leaguers swing in slow motion, it has penetrated into the minds of many, and become a widely used principle for coaches who teach hitting. The problem is, the back elbow doesn't really slot into the body, it drives right past it. The fallacy of the elbow slot has been totally misinterpreted because of the misleading information seen when watching a swing in slow motion.

When you analyze a professional hitter's swing in slow motion, it would appear that the back elbow slots into the body. In fact, when a coach tries to prove this, he will only show this elbow slot occurring. This is the main reason why some people are fooled by the elbow slot fallacy. What is not shown is that the back elbow does not stop at the body but it moves quickly past the body to get the bat head to the desired contact point. The illusion of the elbow slot only occurs when the swing is shown in slow motion and should *never* be taught to hitters.

Matt Zoba

I can usually point out hitters who have been taught to slot their back elbow only by watching a couple of swings. Hitters that are taught to slot the back elbow will usually have three specific swing flaws: 1) lack of bat speed, 2) bad extension, and 3) dragging the barrel head. These flaws occur because their focus is on slotting the back elbow and not getting to the ball quickly.

If a hitter is taught to think about slotting his back elbow instead of attacking the ball with his hands, he will *always* be long to the ball because his hands get left behind. The funny thing is that most coaches who teach hitters to slot their elbow cannot understand why they are consistently long to the ball. The answer is simple: it is because they teach them to slot their elbow.

No good hitter ever thinks about starting his swing with his back elbow. It is always about the hands. In fact, I would bet that the people who teach this absurd idea (if they ever played baseball) never once thought about it when they used to hit. I know for a fact that I never did and do not know anyone else who ever did either. Focusing on slotting the back elbow always slows down the bat speed and will not allow hitters to catch up to any decent pitching.

I really hope that the elbow slot fad is short-lived because teaching it to hitters is truly detrimental. This is a prime example of why coaches must be cautious about what they teach and how they explain it. Incorrect interpretations lead to poor explanations that negatively affect the hitter's performance. Just because something is on video does not mean that it should be taught. Worrying about what the back elbow is doing during the swing is the last thing a hitter needs to be thinking about. The focus must be on driving the hands forward to the ball and the back elbow will naturally do what it does. The elbow slot is one of many misleading principles taught to hitters because of the misinterpreted use of slow motion.

Hips Before Hands

By far, the most common hitting misconception that is taught because of the misuse of slow motion is starting the hips before the hands. The topic has been around for decades and has become a widely accepted hitting assumption throughout baseball and softball. The concept of starting the hips before the hands arises from watching the swing in slow motion. If any Major League swing is broken down in slow motion, it is obvious that the hip rotation *barely* starts forward before the hands do. However, this is something that coaches must not teach hitters.

As I have talked about in previous chapters, the hips play a major role in getting the swing started, and all hitters definitely need to focus on having quick hips to the ball. The most common problem that I have seen with hitters that are taught the hips-before-the-hands philosophy is that when they think about rotating their hips first, their hands normally drag to the ball. The hips-first approach can cause problems with timing by creating a step-by-step process that does not allow fluidity in the swing. These problems will generate serious mechanical swing flaws that greatly affect the hitter's performance on the field.

The proper explanation for using the hips and hands correctly is rather simple. The hitter should *always* think about using his hips and hands together, *never* separately. If he focuses on both the hip rotation and the movement of the hands driving forward together at the same time, the swing will operate more effectively. Anyone who has ever hit knows there is not enough time for the swing to work unless all of the mechanics function together. The swing has to be thought of as a bunch of different parts working in combination to achieve consistent, solid contact. This only happens when hitters are taught to think about the hips and the hands working together as one unit. The swing is not designed to use one without the other, so a hitter should never think about using them at different times.

The biggest thing to remember when teaching hitters to start their hips before their hands is that it only happens in slow motion. The hips-before-hands theory is justified through the use of slow motion but the idea of actually thinking about it during a live swing does not make sense. I have taught hitting for a very long time and seen literally millions of swings. If the swing is seen in normal speed, it is almost impossible to recognize the hips starting before the hands. What *is* easily seen are the hips and hands explosively working together to create maximum bat speed and power behind the ball. Learning how to accurately explain the things seen in slow motion is crucial to give the hitter the proper feedback. Do not let the slow-motion misconception of the hips leading the hands invade the way hitting should be taught.

Locked Front Arm

Recently, I've heard about hitters being taught to lock, or straighten out, their front arm during their swing.

If we were to take random big-leaguers and watch them swing in slow motion, we would see that sometimes the front arm straightens out when their hands start forward. This usually only happens on certain pitches. A locked front arm could occur when the pitch is middle-away, or off-speed, but it is highly unlikely to see it on a fastball inside. Whatever the case, even if it did happen every time a big-leaguer swung the bat (which it doesn't), it is *never* something that should be taught.

Locking out the front arm to start the swing will cause the hitter's front shoulder to pull out and create a longer hand path to the ball. This is probably one of the best examples of how the use of slow motion could be detrimental to a hitter's swing if it is not used properly. Just because a coach finds a slow-motion swing of a big-league hitter who straightens out his front arm when he swings does not mean that it should be focused on or taught. It is something that just happens. What you do not see, because the swing is in slow motion, are the hands attacking the ball out by the hitter's front foot. Driving the hands forward is what the hitter really needs to be thinking about when he swings the bat. When explaining what the hands do during the swing, it should never include locking up the front arm. The primary focus is to create forward momentum with the hands. If any hitter ever thinks about locking out his front arm to start his swing, it will greatly hinder his ability to consistently arrive on time.

A locked front arm does sometimes occur during a Major League swing. However, if you truly care about increasing the success of the hitter, the correct information must be relayed properly. Teaching a locked front arm definitely does not help.

Bat Lag

Bat lag might be the dumbest thing that any coach could ever teach a hitter. Even though I agree 100% that the bat does lag behind the hands during the swing, to teach hitters to lag their bat is comical.

Think about it. A hitter has a fraction of a second to recognize the pitch and decide whether or not to swing at it. Anything that does not help the bat get to the ball quickly will shorten this reaction time and make hitting even harder. I cannot believe that bat lag is even taught, but unfortunately, I do hear it often, even from some credible coaches and misinformed television commentators. This misinterpretation only exists because of a misuse of slow motion.

Watching a Major League swing in slow motion always shows the bat lagging behind the hands. This movement occurs in order for the barrel head to get behind the ball. In fact it is impossible for it *not* to happen when swinging the bat. Bat lag is a function of the swing that happens naturally because the hitter's focus is on driving his hands forward to the ball. However, just because bat lag is easily seen in slow motion (like other misconceptions) does not mean you should teach it. The idea behind teaching the bat to lag is so outrageous that I question why it would even be taught in the first place. A hitter should *never* think about lagging anything to the ball, especially the very thing that has to hit it.

The bat lag seen in slow motion becomes more like bat *drag* when taught to hitters. Teaching hitters to drag their bat to the pitch is flat-out ignorant, unacceptable, and will cause major inconsistencies at the plate. I assume that more advanced hitters will understand the logic behind the bat lagging to the contact point of the pitch, but trying to lag the bat would be counterproductive. The focus should always be on the hands attacking the ball, which will naturally allow the barrel head to arrive on the same plane as the ball. Because of the over-analysis of slow motion, funky things like bat lag end up getting taught. Bat lag is a slow-motion prank on hitting, so do not teach it!

Swing Path

The path that the bat takes to and through the ball is called the *swing path*. There has been a huge debate over the years by coaches with differing hitting philosophies about swing path. I gave my opinion in the first chapter on the problems with these contrasting styles of hitting, but now I am going to show you how the use of slow motion factors in to creating these misleading ideas.

The whole idea of rotational hitting comes from the overuse and over-analysis of slow motion. On the other hand, a lot of the concepts of linear hitting are not even seen in slow motion. In fact, the linear "chopping downhill" motion that is commonly taught by coaches will never be seen in a slow-motion swing of a big-league hitter. Almost all Major League hitters have swings that resemble what the rotational style describes, but

Cody Hastings

they probably *think* about a linear hand path to the ball. What is often seen in slow motion regarding the swing path is not necessarily what should be thought about during the swing.

If a big-league swing is analyzed in slow motion, it will show a very slight uphill swing path through the ball. This is because the pitch is coming out of the pitcher's hand at a slight downhill angle. Since hitters need to get the barrel head behind the ball to consistently hit the ball squarely, there must be a slight upward angle that gets the bat on the same plane as the ball. The slightly uphill swing path seen in slow motion is used by rotational-hitting instructors to defend why they teach what they teach. The problem, however, is not with whether or not this concept is true (because is it very visible in slow motion), but more on the lines of how it is taught and explained to hitters.

Coaches need to use caution when explaining the swing path to hitters. Even though specific things are seen in slow motion, hitters need to understand what to think about in order to allow the proper swing path to happen. All hitters that I have known that were taught the rotational uphill path developed other swing flaws. Some of the common flaws that can occur when hitters think about trying to swing the bat on an uphill plane are: getting long; pulling off; dipping; rolling over; and being late to the ball. These things all happen if hitters are taught the mindset of swinging uphill through the ball.

Instead, hitters need to take the mental approach of attacking the hands forward to the ball and the swing will naturally level out slightly uphill behind the ball. Just because an uphill swing path can sometimes be seen in the slow-motion swing of a big-leaguer, it should not be taught as something that hitters should ever think about. The slow-motion bat path deception is fooling a lot of coaches into teaching false ideas about hitting, which deeply affects the development of the hitter. Are you going to be fooled as well?

Matt Kimmel

The Perfect Swing

After learning about the pros and cons of slow-motion video analysis, I think this is a great time to talk about the main reason why I devoted a whole chapter to this topic, the concept of creating the perfect swing.

In my opinion, the quest for the perfect swing has been the most influential factor in causing misinterpretations of slow-motion video. The common formula for success in developing a great hitter is driven by the attempt to create a perfect swing. Unfortunately, I have bad news. There is no such thing as a perfect swing. In fact, one consistent perfect swing will actually hinder the overall success of a hitter because it forces them to have to hit the ball in the perfect hitting zone *every time*.

If our focus is on developing a perfect swing, we are missing out on a very important aspect of hitting: adjusting the body to the ball. Of course, the goal of every hitter should be to contact the ball in the proper hitting zone, but what if he gets fooled on a pitch? A perfect swing will never allow the hitter to adjust his body to successfully contact the ball on the barrel of the bat. Great hitters become great because they can adjust their body positions during their swing to match the height, location, and velocity of the pitch. To explain it bluntly, hitters must have multiple "perfect" swings. This is one of the brutal realities of hitting. A pitch will fool hitters from time to time, but all awesome hitters have an uncanny ability to still hit the ball hard even when they do not contact the ball in the desired area.

This means hitters must be able to maneuver their body differently to inside pitches vs. outside pitches, higher pitches vs. lower pitches, and pitches that get too deep vs. pitches they get too far out in front on. When a hitter finally comes to the realization that it is impossible to contact the ball in the ideal hitting zone all the time, only then will he learn how to make minor adjustments to the pitch with his body. These forward, backward, in, out, up and down adjustments will tremendously increase the successful contact area from about 1 foot to about 3 feet, which is *huge* for a hitter.

A great example of a perfect swing hindering a hitter's ability is about a player I have trained who could potentially play pro ball. In other words, he is a really, really good player. He came to me during a lesson one day and said that he was struggling with hitting curveballs too far out front. I asked him what his coach was telling him to do. His response was what I would expect to hear from 99% of coaches: "stay back" more with the primary focus on keeping his perfect swing. I started laughing and this player was very confused. I asked him if he realized that focusing on "staying back" was the problem. He looked at me as if I was crazy. I asked him if he had watched any Major League games lately and he obviously had. Then I asked him a question that completely changed his whole perspective about hitting curveballs. I simply asked him what does he see big-leaguers do when they are out front on an off-speed pitch? He replied in a joking way that they lunge at it. I smiled back and told him that next time that he sees a curveball to do the same. He called me back that night after his game and said he went 3-for-3 with three doubles, all off of curveballs.

This is a prime example of the imperfections of a perfect swing. Of course the goal of a hitter is not to lunge at the ball, but the reality of hitting is that you must be able to naturally adjust your body during your swing. If you don't believe this, watch any big-league game and count for yourself how many times hitters do not contact the pitch in the proper hitting zone but still find a way to get hits. It was unbelievable to me and I was completely amazed when I first noticed it.

On top of that, I have never seen or heard of a coach or player *ever* work on this important aspect of hitting. They are always too busy searching for secrets (usually using slow motion) to enhance their already perfect swing, never realizing that they are severely limiting their hitting ability. At some point, all coaches and hitters must think about what their real intentions are: to create a perfect swing or to improve on field results?

If used correctly, slow-motion swing analysis can definitely help a hitter's in-game success. If used incorrectly, it will definitely help a hitter manufacture a perfect swing.

Bottom of the 6th

The use of slow motion can be very helpful for hitters if it is used correctly. To get the full benefit of slow motion, analyze live game at-bats. Take into consideration the outside influences that affect what you're seeing. Be careful not to compare all hitters to one specific Major League swing, and do not use video to try to clone hitters.

My personal experience leads me to believe that slow motion is misused more often than not. Because of the over-analysis of slow motion, it is often forgotten that the hitter's swing should be explosive and quick. The focus gets placed on irrelevant parts of the swing that hitters should never think about. I wrote this chapter to clear up some of the misconceptions that slow motion can create and to give an idea of what really should be taught.

For hitters to get the most out of slow-motion swing analysis, they must learn the overall principles given in this chapter. Only then will they be able to identify and fix their real problems. Remember, the goal is to become a better hitter, not to just create a perfect swing!

End of the Inning

The purpose of using slow motion is to help identify specific problems of each individual hitter, not to manufacture swings that all look identical.

Chapter 6

No Such Thing as a Softball Swing

Is there a difference between hitting a baseball and a fast-pitch softball?

Since the subtitle of this book is "The Brutal Reality of Hitting," prepare yourself for the ultimate truth about what needs to be taught about hitting and fast-pitch softball. If you are a fast-pitch softball player, parent, or coach, you probably have not heard a lot about what I'm going to talk about in this chapter. That's because much of what fast-pitch hitters are taught is not only wrong, it's ridiculous. I think the primary reason for bad instruction comes from the misconception that baseball and softball are two different games. Yes, there probably is more small-ball on the softball field, but other than that, the games are not so different.

The last time I checked, almost everything about baseball and softball is the same except for the pitching distance, the distance between the base paths, the distance to the fences, and some obvious minor rule variations (which I do not feel a need to cover). The different dimensions of the field do not change anything about hitting.

In fact, let me clear up one major fallacy about distance and fast-pitch softball: fast-pitch softball hitters do not have less time to react to the pitch. I have heard many times that because the pitcher is so much closer to home plate, hitters have less time to react, so their swing should be different than a baseball swing. This is not true (and even if it were, the swing would still not be any different).

A good pitcher at the high-school varsity level can throw the ball around 60 mph. With the mound distance at 43 feet, a 60-mph softball pitch equates to about an 87-mph baseball pitch from 60 feet (which is a good velocity, as well, for a high school varsity baseball player). The same is true for college and professional players. In fast-pitch softball, a good college pitcher will throw a fastball in the mid to upper 60s. This equates to a mid to upper 90s fastball in baseball, which is exactly what a good college pitcher will throw. Since pitchers in fast-pitch softball and baseball have about the same release-point distance of approximately 6 extra feet, it does not factor into comparing the overall reaction time for the batter. So baseball and softball hitters have roughly the same amount of time to react to the pitch regardless of the level of play.

Another misconception is that baseball and softball swings should be different because of the differing heights of the pitcher's release point. This stems from the idea that because the fast-pitch softball release point is so much lower, the movements of the pitches are totally different—because the ball moves in different ways, the swing must also move in a different way. This fallacy explains why some softball coaches think fast-pitch girls must have different swings than boys playing baseball. This cannot be further from the truth.

The only "different" pitch in fast-pitch softball is the rise ball, but even in baseball, there are sidearmers who throw a pitch with similar movement (I detail how to hit rise balls later in this chapter). All other pitches have pretty close to the same movements. A fastball on the softball diamond is the same as a fastball in baseball, just a little flatter. A change-up has the same floating and sinking action. A fast-pitch curveball is either a slider or a cutter on the baseball field. Drop-balls have the same sinking effect as any good two-seam fastball. Screwballs move in on the hitter like any left-handed pitcher throwing a fastball in to a right-handed hitter. Hitters in softball see almost the exact same pitch movements—going to the exact same strike zone—as a baseball hitter, only from a lower release point. For this reason, the swing mechanics are the same for both fast-pitch softball and baseball.

Hitting is Hitting

Still, I've seen some crazy things taught in the softball world, by revered coaches and hitting instructors. These include rolling the hands over at contact; finishing the swing low; and not rotating the hips at all. There are countless other wacky ideas that aren't even worth mentioning. These outrageous theories are rooted in the idea that hitting in fast-pitch softball is totally different than hitting in baseball.

There is no such thing as a "softball swing." To say that there is a difference between hitting a fast-pitch softball and a baseball is laughable and shows ignorance of what hitting is all about. It's also unfortunate, because it limits girls in their overall potential as a hitter.

Don't get me wrong. I know softball coaches who do a great job of teaching hitting. Most high-level NCAA Division I coaches understand that hitting is hitting, whether the pitch is thrown underhand or overhand. My problem is not with these coaches, nor with the average parent-volunteer, but with coaches who try to fool people with ludicrous ways of teaching fast-pitch softball players how to hit. It needs to stop.

There are too many self-proclaimed fast-pitch hitting instructors promoting bogus philosophies. They limit the hitter's potential by teaching off-the-wall mechanics, and worse, giving absolutely no instruction on the right mentality or approach at the plate. Too often, hitting instructors focus on the function of the swing (which is usually taught wrong anyway) and not on the things that actually make hitters better.

If we really do care about these athletes' future and want to help them get the most out of their abilities, there needs to be a transformation in hitting instruction for fast-pitch softball players. This transformation starts by getting rid of the idea that the softball swing is somehow different. It's not. The bat speed, mentality,

Bridget Raftery

plan, approach, and adjustment parts of hitting that were taught in Chapters 3, 4, and 5 are for fast-pitch softball players as well.

These aspects of hitting are greatly overlooked in the softball world. In my opinion, this is the primary reason why there is so much more "small ball" in softball. Since girls unfortunately are not taught the things that can make them better hitters, they tend not to have very good results on the field and coaches resort to using small ball to score runs. Coaches and hitting instructors need to stop listening to the popular (but ineffective) schools of thought regarding softball hitting instruction and start teaching hitting correctly. In doing so, fast-pitch softball players can begin to perform to their greatest potential at the plate.

Do not be the one to limit this potential by trying to reinvent the swing. I consistently see girls who have serious problems at the plate because what they are taught ignores the truth about hitting. Fortunately, I've seen amazing improvements in hitters once they have a chance to maximize their full potential. Whether you're a coach or a player, this chapter will help you to understand the "not so" differences in baseball and softball. However, to really understand what it takes to be a hitter, that information is in the rest of this book.

The "Not So" Differences

I want to make it very clear that whether you're hitting a softball or a baseball, the swing mechanics and mental approach are exactly the same. However, there are important non-mechanical differences that are *never* mentioned in the softball community. What follows will be new information for most people but very beneficial to coaches and the overall development for girls who play fast-pitch.

Shelby McCannel

Swing Path

The swing path is the same in softball and baseball. There are, however, slight swing-path differences depending on the height and movement of different pitches. Whether these pitches are coming from a higher or lower release point does not matter. The swing path in both fast-pitch softball and baseball must take the same approach of arriving on time and on plane to the ball. It does not matter what type of pitch it is, where it is moving, or what velocity it is thrown at. Hitters who consistently get their barrel plane behind the ball at contact will square more balls up more often.

This is where the misconception of swinging down to the ball comes from in softball. Because pitchers throw a rise ball, a lot of coaches think hitters have to swing down to the ball. A hitter who consistently chops down through the ball will not be able to keep the barrel head on the same plane as ball on different pitches. Chopping down might allow her to hit a high pitch occasionally, but not much else. Teaching hitters to chop down to the ball for the sake of being able to hit an occasional rise ball greatly limits their overall hitting ability.

Arista Honey

Speaking of rise balls, let's talk about some things you need to know about hitting them. First of all, a rise ball is a high fastball. It might give the effect of "rising" to the hitter, but players must approach it the same way baseball players would when hitting a high fastball. With any high pitch, the hitter's goal is not to hit it but to lay off it. Laying-off the rise ball is hard because the lower release point makes it look like a strike as it leaves the pitcher's hand. Just because the pitch looks like a strike does not give the hitter an excuse to swing. A lot of pitches look like strikes but end up out of the strike zone.

Being able to lay off the rise ball obviously has to do with pitch recognition. However, I believe there is a huge problem with the approach players are taught. Many coaches tell hitters to move up in the box when the pitcher throws a lot of rise balls so they can hit the ball before it rises. I totally disagree with this idea. When you move up in the box, the rise ball will look more like a strike as it leaves the pitcher's hand, and a good rise ball is really hard to hit. By moving back in the box, the hitter is able to see the ball longer, which gives her a better opportunity to let it go for a ball, which is the goal. If the hitter does make the decision to swing at the pitch, the bat's swing path should be slightly downward (which is true in baseball as well).

To say that fast-pitch softball players require a different swing path to the ball is completely false. Uneducated coaches who teach players to chop down or roll the hands over at contact usually do so because of misleading information about hitting rise balls. These made-up hitting philosophies originate with the sole purpose of trying to teach hitters how to hit one pitch, in one location.

Remember that the rise ball is only one of many pitches that move on different planes. In order to be able to hit *all* pitches, the hitter must consistently get the barrel head of the bat squared up behind the ball. This will not happen if hitters are continually taught incorrect theories about the swing path.

Eyes Focused Downhill

The one real difference for hitters in fast-pitch softball compared to baseball is where the eyes need to focus. This is *never* talked about in softball but is of the utmost importance. If the hitter's eyes start in the right spot, they will see the ball better, make quicker pitch-recognition decisions, lay off rise balls (or bad pitches in general), and duplicate proper swing mechanics. By doing this one simple but very helpful thing, hitters can instantly give themselves a better opportunity for success.

In baseball, the pitcher's release point is usually above the shoulder. The pitcher also stands on a mound, forcing the hitter's eyes to focus slightly uphill to see the pitch. In softball, it's the opposite: the pitcher stands on flat ground, with the release point of the pitch somewhere between the hip and the knee. In softball, training the hitter's head and eyes slightly downhill, toward the pitcher's knee or hip, focuses her vision on the most opportune spot to recognize pitches.

This sounds easy enough to do, but there is one major obstacle that makes it hard to accomplish: the facemask. It often impedes the hitter's vision.

Facemasks in fast-pitch softball are necessary for safety; however, they also obstruct the hitter in two ways. The first is that because the facemask covers below the chin, it is almost impossible for the hitter to keep her head down during contact. Through the swing, the back shoulder moves forward and hits the bottom of the mask, which forces the head to come up too early. I call it the "softball head."

The other reason deals with why the hitter starts with her head and eyes focused more uphill. The horizontal bars on the facemask can obstruct the hitter's vision. In an effort to see the pitch through an opening between the bars, she has to tilt her head and eyes more at an uphill angle, which leads to poor pitch recognition and bad swing habits. Coaches almost always overlook this but it is an easy problem to fix. To start, make the hitter get in her stance and focus her eyes slightly downhill. Then, pull the facemask down until her eyes can see through the mask without the bar impeding her sight. When the hitter has a slight angle of her head tilted downhill and there are no obstacles getting in the way of her vision, it will be easier for her to recognize pitches.

Where the eyes focus is the only real difference in hitting a softball versus a baseball. Keeping the eyes looking downhill, at the release point, does not mean the swing should change mechanically. Simply put, focus on changing the angle of the eyes, not on transforming the whole swing.

Slapping

Slapping has become a huge part of fast-pitch softball. A good slapper can change the outcome of the game and put enormous pressure on the defense. My goal for this section is to give a truthful perspective on what it takes to be a great slapper and to clear up some common misunderstandings. I am not going to get into detailed slapping techniques because most coaches talk too much about mechanics when teaching slapping and don't allow the hitter's athleticism take over. When instruction gets too mechanical, slapping becomes more of a robotic five-step process. This hinders the player's ability to understand what needs to happen for slapping to truly be effective.

There are specific characteristics that a player must possess to become a productive slapper. Unfortunately, the one most coaches look for is a lack of production at the plate. It is very common in the softball world to try to make a struggling hitter into a slapper.

To be brutally honest, most of the time difficulties with hitting are directly caused by the same mechanically focused coaches trying to turn players into slappers. While I agree that some players cannot hit no matter how good

Morgan Figueroa

the instruction, this does not mean they should be automatically made into a slapper. The reality is that not everyone can slap.

All great slappers must have crazy speed and an ability to comfortably transfer their hand-eye coordination over to the other side of the plate (if they are not naturally left handed).

In all of my years of teaching hitting, only once did I recommend that a girl try slapping. She was an average hitter from the right side but absolutely flew when she ran. Her hope was to play at the college level, but there was no chance for that as a right-handed hitter. Because speed was her greatest asset, I told her that if she wanted to have a chance to play college ball, she needed to become a slapper. She tried it and felt very comfortable from the left side of the plate. After learning the correct technique, she has had tremendous success. Her success, however, did not come from mechanics but from how fast she ran to first base. She now plays at the college level because she is productively utilizing her speed. If a player isn't fast, slapping is probably not for her and she should work hard on being a better hitter instead.

Since it has been established that the main characteristics needed for slapping are speed and hand-eye coordination from the left side, I am now going to cover the most important things that make great slappers:

Getting on base: Slappers must be patient at the plate and not swing at balls out of the strike zone. Drawing a walk is always just as good as a slap hit.

Establishing the bunt: Drag bunting makes slapping effective. If a slapper can drag-bunt to both sides of the field, the defense has to play in closer to take the bunt away. With the corners in, the slapper has a better opportunity to find a hole in the infield. When the player can add a soft drag bunt to the slapping game, it is almost impossible to defend.

Lauren Brown

Placing the ball: The ideal spot for the slapper to place the ball is right past the third baseman, into the six-hole, but each situation will be determined by the defense and location of the pitch. Really good slappers can place the ball wherever they want. They can chop it into the ground for a higher bounce, move it left or right of the third baseman and shortstop, or even hit it up the middle or pull it when the defense allows for it. Placement of the ball will usually dictate whether or not the slapper will reach first base safely.

Generating momentum: The last thing that all great slappers must do is to generate maximum momentum out of the box toward first base as contact is being made. This means the slapper must be running at full speed as quickly as possible after contact. It does not matter if the player drag bunts or a slaps, her momentum out of the box plays a major role in being safe or out at first base.

Most slappers I see do not get a good jump out of the box because they are taught to move mechanically rather than quickly and instinctively. There is one specific foot placement commonly taught that greatly hinders the slapper's momentum toward first. After the right foot takes a small jab-step back toward the left foot, the left foot crosses over the right foot, starting the momentum forward. The problem occurs when slappers are taught that when the left foot crosses over, the toes should be pointing toward home plate. This is the main misconception with slapping. When the foot is pointing towards the plate, the slapper cannot turn her hips to generate momentum toward first. The left foot should be directed more toward the pitcher while the shoulders stay straight, not flying open. Everything in the upper body should stay the same, as if the player were hitting. The only difference is that the ball will travel deeper.

The mechanics of slapping are a much more detailed than this. I chose not to cover everything because I want the focus to be on things that normally are not taught about slapping. The problems I see regularly are

Andi Hormel

easily fixed. Speed, hand-eye coordination, establishing the drag bunt, placement of the ball, and momentum out of the box are the *real* things that make great slappers. Although proper mechanics are important, they are definitely over-taught by coaches. Players need to be given some freedom to let their athleticism take over. Do not box them up by getting too mechanical! It will truly impede their ability to perform.

Bottom of the 7th

To be a great hitter in fast-pitch softball, players need to take the same mental and mechanical approach as in baseball. There are numerous reasons why the swing works the way it does, and guess what? I didn't make them up. The widely accepted, mainstream hitting mechanics of today apply to both baseball and softball. There is no difference. If a hitter wants to compete at a high level, she must take the overall principles from the other chapters in this book and put them into play.

It is extremely upsetting to know that the majority of fast-pitch softball players will never hit to their full potential because of the coaching they receive on swing mechanics. While swing mechanics are important, there is so much more to hitting than what the swing is supposed to look like. Fast-pitch players at the lower levels through high school are rarely taught about the mentality, plan, and approach. If coaches truly want to develop hitters and maximize their capabilities, they first need to break away from the misleading principles circulating about hitting. The softball world is in dire need of a serious change. A change like this can only happen by starting at the foundation. In this case, the foundation is an understanding that hitting in baseball and fast-pitch softball is the same. The next time someone tells you there is a difference between a baseball and a softball swing, do not listen to them, because what they just said exposes their lack of knowledge in teaching hitting!

End of the Inning

There are no differences between a baseball and a softball swing.
In fact, there is no such thing as a softball swing in the first place!

Chapter 7

8th Inning

A Coach's Guide to Hitting

Putting it all together: Knowledge, credibility, and strategy

After reading the majority of this book, do you think you have enough knowledge to teach someone how to hit? I think you do. Would that knowledge alone give you the ability to help a hitter achieve consistent, quality results on the field? I'd have to say no, because there is much more to quality hitting instruction than knowing what to teach.

The ability to teach hitting begins with knowledge of hitting. That said, knowledge alone won't give you the capacity to be a great hitting coach. The key is to combine knowledge with an understanding of how specific things should be taught and explained. Remember that the foundational concept to proper hitting instruction is to give the hitter what he needs by identifying his real problems and then relaying correct information properly.

Learning to give hitters what they truly need takes an enormous amount of time. Just imagine how long it's taken me to get to where I am at now. I played nine years of baseball from t-ball through junior high, and then four years in high school, four years in college, and about six more years in pro ball. That tallies up to 23 years of playing. During that time I had the opportunity to learn from some of the best coaches in America. When I retired from playing, I felt like I had a tremendous amount of knowledge that I could pass along.

Boy, was I wrong. I had experience and prerequisite knowledge, but I was not very good at relaying information. I had no idea how to give individual players what they really needed. I was one year removed from playing professional baseball and couldn't even help 14-year-olds improve their hitting. At the time, I taught basic mainstream swing mechanics that made them look better, but never truly enhanced their skills. The funny thing is that the main hitting concepts I taught 10 years ago, I don't even teach anymore because they're pretty much insignificant.

So here I am, 10 years into my career as a professional hitting instructor, writing a book on hitting, and man, have my ways of teaching changed. Over those years, I've spent an unbelievable number of hours studying hitting in an effort to gain more wisdom and understanding about how to *really* help hitters. What's helped me most is the time I have spent giving instruction. Year-round, my daily work consists of personal instruction, coaching teams, working with all skill levels and ages of both boys and girls, and, most importantly, dealing with different personalities and learning abilities. Regularly coaching such a variety of athletes has given me the ability to understand how hitting is truly supposed to be taught. Hopefully, I will look back 10 years from now and see a progression of learning that has given me an even better understanding of what hitters really need.

A Logical Teaching Progression

I see a lot of coaches today who are just like I was and that's why I am so passionate about this book. My goal is to explain what it takes to be a quality hitting coach so others don't make the same mistakes that I made and obstruct a player's full potential at the plate. I'm not trying to make everyone a hitting expert, but for those coaches who have the desire to make their players better, this section will help you teach your players how to improve their hitting.

Let me start with a list of what should be taught. How quickly you progress through these stages depends greatly on the hitter, but the basic principles of hitting should be covered in this approximate order:

1. Controlling the proper mechanics and timing of the swing.
2. Maximizing bat speed.
3. Hitting fastballs in all areas of the strike zone.
4. Pitch selection.
5. Hitting off-speed pitches.
6. Pitch recognition.
7. Hitting mixed up pitches at different speeds.
8. Making adjustments.
9. Plan and approach.
10. Situational hitting.
11. Challenging hitters beyond their normal capabilities.

The order of these fundamentals may be altered slightly, and the mental aspects of hitting can be taught at any point you find necessary. But this progression should allow coaches at any level to give their hitters what they need based upon where they are in their development. I, personally, as well as the staff at Rijo Athletics, have used this progression for years and it is the most effective process in developing hitters.

If a coach uses this basic progression outline as a foundation for instruction, there will always be something new for a hitter to work on. Coaches who can continually present new ways to help hitters improve will encourage them to work on their hitting regularly. I see a lot of hitters who burn out because they do the same boring things all the time, with no real excitement in their training. I think most of this boredom and burnout stems from a coach's inability to help hitters progress.

Now, if you're a coach with beginner or intermediate hitters, you will probably stick to teaching the first basic principle for years, and I can understand that it may seem monotonous if the hitter isn't improving mechanically. But even when dealing with hitters who need a lot of mechanical work, coaches can and should devise specific plans to help them mechanically while keeping the instruction new and exciting.

If you coach more advanced hitters, go ahead and work on multiple principles at once because this, too, will keep the workouts fresh. In fact, all hitters at some point will need to go back and work on every point in this progression. The reasoning for the order of this outline is that, as the hitter improves in his training, the coach's level of instruction must advance as well. As coaches, we should never get to a point where the level of instruction comes to a standstill. Remember, no matter what age or ability you're coaching, there is *always* something hitters need.

Relaying Information to Hitters

After understanding the progression of how hitting should be taught, all great coaches must be able to explain these concepts correctly. In all honesty, this is where a lot of coaches fail miserably. Most coaches understand the basic form and function of the swing but struggle to relay the correct information and to explain things properly. In fact, there is an abundance of incorrect information and/or explanations given in most hitting instruction today.

Unfortunately, there is no magic formula to help coaches give the right information in the right way to hitters. Coaches must start by gaining enough knowledge and then putting that knowledge to the test through

David Oppenheim

trial and error. With experience, you'll gain wisdom about how things should be explained. That's pretty much how I learned. The only difference is that I had the opportunity to learn from my mistakes at a much faster pace because of the number of hours I put in doing hitting lessons every day.

When it comes to relaying information, coaches should always make recommendations instead of forcing hitters to do certain things. These recommendations should be based on the individual hitter's needs with the intent to address his specific problems. If a suggestion is not working or the player doesn't like it, then the coach must try something else. All great hitting instructors have the ability to adapt and explain the same concepts in different ways. They're also able to give good reasons why certain things are taught and how they help each player individually.

Make sure to only recommend things if they need fixing and be careful not to over-teach. If it ain't broke, then don't fix it. Hitting is hitting. There will always be new philosophies and ideas, but the foundational concepts of hitting will not change. The only thing that should change is how the information is relayed, with the coach adapting to each hitter's needs.

Traits of Successful Hitting Coaches

Let's get into some of the characteristics that all hitting coaches need in order to be successful. I can go on and on about every attribute, but I will try to focus on what is most important:

Experience: If you played college or professional baseball, you have an obvious advantage because of your ability to understand the concepts and intricacies of hitting. Your experience also brings credibility. You have a

Nick Pribble

"respect-factor" with your players before anything is even taught. That said, just because you played at a high level doesn't automatically make you a great hitting coach. I know too many coaches who played college or pro ball and have no clue how to teach hitting.

On the contrary, I'm sure there are hitting coaches who never played college ball or beyond and do a great job developing hitters. For those coaches who maybe didn't play at a high level, respect must be earned by producing consistent results on the field.

Physical capabilities: Because players are more likely to pay attention to someone who can actually hit, this leads to another important trait of a good hitting coach: being able to properly demonstrate what you're trying to teach. If at all possible, I highly recommend that coaches stay in shape and work on their own swings so they can show what certain things are supposed to look like. Even though I have been retired for more than 10 years now, I make a constant effort to work on my own hitting. Trust me, it helps. What player will listen to a coach who can't swing properly? It sounds funny, but it's true. Would you take golf lessons from someone who isn't good at golf? Or hire a personal trainer who never works out and eats nothing but fast food? The same goes for hitting. If your own hitting needs work, then work at it. A coach who can hit and properly demonstrate hitting will always earn more credibility, respect, and trust from his players.

Confidence: Just as players need confidence at the plate, a coach must be confident in what he is teaching. When I first started giving hitting instruction, I would stumble over phrases and explanations because I didn't feel confident in what I was trying to teach. This was a huge barrier in my ability to give quality instruction. It wasn't until several years later that I finally felt 100% confident in what I was teaching and how I was teaching it. If a coach cannot confidently relay what he's trying to teach, hitters will see through it quickly and

Steffen Torgersen

lose interest in what is being taught. A coach must exude an aura of confidence in order for his players to believe that what he's teaching will be beneficial to them. Believe in what you teach and know what you teach. If you don't, your players won't either.

Enthusiasm and energy: These are essential for coaches who want to get the most out of their players. Have fun and enjoy teaching, because the more energy you have, the more likely the athlete will want to learn. Don't be the coach who sits on a bucket with a dull and boring attitude, giving the perception of being uninterested. Instead, show excitement when a hitter does something right. High-fives, chest bumps, or even a simple hug can make a lasting impression. Your energy tells players that you care about their development. If you cannot be enthusiastic, then you should probably ask yourself why you're coaching.

Positive actions and attitude: There are many other important traits a hitting coach must have. Patience, honesty, attentiveness, and kindness come to mind. If we were all perfect coaches, I guess we'd possess every positive attribute, but we are not. Our actions, positive and negative, will influence every athlete we coach. Be careful how you say and do things. Coaching is about more than just hitting and baseball. We are role models.

The basic formula for success is to challenge hitters who need to be challenged and to encourage hitters who need encouragement. Most hitters need a little of both. Find out what works for each person and provide the correct information and approach based upon his individual needs, not what worked for you.

Time and effort: Becoming a coach who can really help hitters improve takes serious time and effort. You need to put it all together: to understand and follow the teaching progression; identify each individual's strengths and weaknesses; gain the knowledge to address them; be able to relay information in a way the hitter will comprehend; and personally develop the characteristics that will help you become a more informed, respected, and credible coach.

This is the recipe for success when it comes to teaching hitting. Be patient in the process, because learning how to teach hitting properly takes just as much time as learning how to hit. It's also a never-ending process for the more serious coach!

Consistency in Training

Consistency in training with repetitions done right is mandatory for any hitter who wants to be the best he can possibly be. It takes a long time to become a quality hitter, and for the serious athlete who wants to play at the college or professional level, development is a continuous process. Even the guys in the big-leagues, playing at the highest level possible, are always looking for ways to get better. These players take batting practice almost every day from spring training through the end of their season, which lasts about eight months or even longer if they go deep into the post-season. Obviously, these guys get paid to play baseball and it is their job to hit every day. We can't expect Little Leaguers or high school kids to train as often or as hard as the pros do. But the idea here is that hitters who train consistently and iron out wrinkles in their game through tiresome repetition are more likely to find success at the plate.

The lack of consistent training has been one of the most frustrating things that I have dealt with during my coaching career. I have worked with countless athletes who could have been extraordinary hitters but never achieved their full potential because they didn't work on their hitting consistently. They didn't have the desire to spend that much time practicing, didn't completely understand how much effort had to go into being a great hitter, or thought they already had it all figured out. In any case, hitting is not something that players can work on occasionally and expect to attain consistent desirable results. It is just too hard.

In fact, I've worked with numerous hitters who did not have a lot of ability when they started but were able to play college and even pro ball because they stuck to a plan of steady training. It took several years of almost year-round training to develop the abilities they needed for a chance to play at those levels, and even more of a commitment once they got there. Their work ethic gave them the opportunity to play at these levels, and consistent work was the key to their success.

In-Season Training

The first thing about in-season training that hitters need to know is that they need to do it. I've heard a lot of excuses over the years for not being able to train in-season, the most common one being that because of games and practices there isn't enough time. My response is that serious and committed players make time to work on their hitting because they know how important it is.

Another reason why players don't work on hitting as often as they should during the season is because they think there is no need to do it. They feel they hit enough with their team and so in-season training is not necessary. This cannot be farther from the truth. In-season hitting instruction is extremely important. In fact, it's vital to continue to train throughout the season. I've see many hitters work hard during the off-season and start their regular season hot at the plate, only to cool down because they failed to continue to train. Slumps and struggles are easier to fix if the player stays consistent with his hitting.

Knowing exactly what to work on during the season is important. The best way to get immediate results starts with working on the hitter's mental approach and timing. Making minor timing and approach adjustments will help lead the hitter in the right direction.

Remember, the main purpose of in-season hitting work should be to try and quickly fix specific problems. If the hitter has mechanical problems during the season, focus on making *minor* mechanical adjustments. In my experience, making major mechanical changes to a swing during the season does not help. Most of the time, it only makes things worse because the hitter ends up thinking way too much. In fact, bad swing mechanics will improve just by changing the hitter's approach. Be careful about changing swing mechanics during the season.

The overall idea with in-season hitting instruction is to quickly identify problems and make minor adjustments, both mentally and physically. If the hitter isn't struggling, then he shouldn't change a thing. Instead, he should work on his approach, recognizing different pitches, hitting different pitches to different areas of the strike zone, and making whatever refinements are necessary to retain his performance. Focus on quality repetitions done right during the season, and make an effort to get in extra hitting work.

Off-Season Training

Once the season is over, players should take a little time off from the game to get rejuvenated and to reflect on what went well and what needs to improve. Assessing the hitter's strengths and weaknesses at this point will help him develop a training plan and be more efficient with his off-season workouts.

How hard and consistently a hitter works during the off-season plays a huge role in determining his in-season results. The off-season is the best time for hitters to make changes to their swing or their approach. A swing overhaul can take a long time to get comfortable with. If the player's hitting needs a serious overhaul, he has more time to become familiar with the changes in the off-season. Also, with fewer games being played at this time of year, major mechanical or mental adjustments are easier to achieve without the pressure of competition.

The off-season is a great time to use specific hitting tools and drills to fix individual problems as well as improve bat speed and power. Wood bats, certain weighted bats, and other tools can help improve hand-eye coordination, swing mechanics, balance, body control, and confidence (just to name a few). Hitters must use this time of year to do whatever it takes to focus on individual weaknesses while continuing to work on *all* aspects of hitting.

For the more serious athlete, there is no off-season. When the final game of the season is over, it's time for a hitter to refocus, recommit, and reestablish their dedication to achieving his ultimate hitting potential.

Coaching Batting Practice

The approach to batting practice should be dictated by each individual's needs. Often, however, this is not the case.

One of the biggest mistakes coaches make during batting practice is to make their whole team use the same approach. Some coaches will have their whole team focus on hitting the ball to the opposite field, while others have players work on hitting the ball on the ground. Whatever the case, coaches must be careful how they approach batting practice.

Remember that hitting is an individual aspect of a team sport. All hitters have different abilities and each hitter will have his own strengths and weaknesses. Don't get me wrong, I agree that hitters must be able to hit the ball to all fields or on the ground (or whatever else the coach desires), and I am in no way downplaying the importance of working on hit-and-runs, situational hitting, moving runners over, etc. My objection is that it doesn't help each player's individual weaknesses. In fact, I've seen a lot of hitters develop swing flaws because the coach made them do things during BP that actually made their individual problems worse.

Austin Baek

Branden Kelliher

An example of this is a team I used to train a while back. I worked with this team a little bit during the off-season but also with a lot of the players individually. After a short time, I began to see that some of the hitters had regressed and were having trouble getting the barrel head out front on pitches middle-in. They were able to hit the ball the other way pretty well but had no chance to hit any fastball inside. So I asked the players what their coach had them to do during team batting practice and the answer was to hit everything to the opposite field. That made total sense, since they were struggling to hit average batting practice fastballs. Unknowingly, the coach's team hitting approach was starting to affect a lot of hitters individually.

Fortunately, a few of the players were able to adjust back to their individual strengths and have success. However, others struggled mightily. The last thing they needed was to be told to hit the ball the opposite way because they already couldn't catch up to a good fastball and had no chance at squaring up an inside pitch. Instead, they needed to learn how to contact the ball more out front and pull it rather than letting it travel deeper. Their swing flaws were caused by a team philosophy that damaged their individual approach. The goal of every coach should be to help each player individually, which in turn, will tremendously help the team.

This is a great example because it leads into one of my biggest pet peeves: the "oppo first" approach to hitting. When a hitter is taught to always work on hitting the ball to the opposite field, he will usually struggle to hit a good fastball and definitely to hit inside pitches. My philosophy is to teach hitters how to get the barrel head out and pull the ball first, especially early in the teaching process. They can learn how to hit the ball to the opposite field after they can consistently make contact out front. I do not encourage teaching hitters to pull every pitch, but as the hitter matures it is harder to learn how to pull the ball than to learn how to hit the ball the other way. Again, this approach is dictated by the individual hitter's needs and what type of hitter they are. But from my daily observation over the years, most hitters (against good pitching) struggle more with getting the ball out front, rather than letting it travel.

Since the overall approach to batting practice should be based on each hitter's needs, coaches must use good judgment depending on the age and skill set of the hitter. They must discern when they can challenge the hitter a bit and when they need to throw the ball into their barrel. If you're dealing with a younger team or an individual who needs a lot of work at the plate, batting practice should be done with the purpose of creating confidence. Coaches should do all they can to encourage these players and build them up, helping them to establish a confident mindset. Live batting practice for beginner or intermediate hitters should start out easy and then, as improvements are made, they can be challenged more and more. One of the worst things a coach can do for less advanced hitters is make BP too hard. It's discouraging and detrimental to their individual development.

On the contrary, live batting practice for a more advanced hitter should not be easy. I understand that there are times where hitters need what I call "wheelhouse BP," where the coach just needs to throw the ball in his wheelhouse to help the hitter feel good about himself. However, I think hitters take too much wheelhouse BP. Great hitters usually don't lack confidence, and most of the time they need to be pushed rather than patted on the back. In fact, if a hitter truly wants to be great, he needs to be pushed beyond his normal abilities and work on things that are much tougher than your typical BP. Making things harder in batting practice will help make the game at-bats easier.

Advanced hitters, no matter the age, must also be put in pressurized game-like situations. In my opinion, this does not happen enough. If a hitter never works consistently on dealing with the stress-and-anxiety part of hitting during practice, he'll have a hard time dealing with it when the game is on the line and his team needs him to clutch up. A lot of our inter-squad practice games in college were more intense than some of our real games, and our whole team quickly learned how to compete in any atmosphere with controlled emotions.

Because our coach held such a high standard in practice by putting pressure on the players to perform, the natural nervousness of hitting became easier to manage.

I think most hitters misunderstand the real purpose of batting practice and spend their time just going through the motions. Instead, BP should be done with a strict plan and purpose. The intent should be to fix specific problems and ambitiously push hitters to a higher standard. Players who sincerely have the desire to improve their hitting need to take a more diligent approach to their batting practice. In doing so, more desirable results will happen more consistently.

In-Game Hitting Instruction

One of the biggest problems I see during games is when coaches say too much about swing mechanics. They talk to their hitters during an at-bat in an effort to help fix a specific mechanical flaw.

Now, obviously a lot of this depends on the age and skill set of the hitter. For younger hitters, it's probably OK to mention some mechanical things occasionally, but for advanced hitters, coaches should focus on helping them with their approach. Most of the time, talking to a hitter about mechanical stuff during his at-bats is detrimental because it makes him think too much at the plate.

An example of this is when a hitter rolls over a pitch that goes foul to his pull side. Most coaches react by telling the hitter that he rolled over and that he needs to get more extension through the ball. However, telling the hitter to focus on hitting the ball hard up the middle or to the opposite side of the field would be a better choice of words. This helps the hitter develop the right approach rather than start thinking about how to fix his swing right there during the at-bat. Better yet, bite your tongue and let the player figure it out himself, especially your better hitters.

Swing mechanics *never* get fixed during a game. The time to work on mechanical issues is in the cage. If a hitter needs a reminder, it's OK to talk between innings or while he's on deck, but coaches should focus on plan, approach, and making adjustments during the game. Save the mechanical coaching for practice when there is more time to break down the swing.

Another problem is parents trying to give hitting instruction to their kids. If you are a parent reading this book, please listen to me clearly because this may be the most vital information you ever receive about talking to your kids during a game. The only things parents should say to their kids during a game are encouraging words. Encourage them when they strike out and praise them when they get a hit. From my own experience, most of what parents say in an effort to help their kids only makes things worse. Trust me on this. I have taught hitting for a long time, and parents unknowingly do more harm to their child's hitting than help it.

As hard as it may be, parents should leave the teaching to the coach, even if the coach isn't that knowledgeable. You parents who played baseball at a high level and know a little bit about hitting, this goes for you, too. I have seen players who after every pitch would turn and look into the stands at their dads for help instead of checking with their coach for the sign. This is disrespectful to the coach as well as to the team and ruins the flow of the game. If you're a parent and feel the need to say something to your kid, save it for another time.

A better idea would be to go to the game and just enjoy watching your child having fun playing the game he loves. Letting the athlete try to figure it out himself a bit during the game will only benefit his future!

Bottom of the 8th

My hope is that after reading this book, coaches will have a more thorough understanding of how to explain things to their hitters correctly. I also hope that players will have a better perspective on what it takes to become a quality hitter. The only way this is achieved is to commit as much time as possible to learning, studying, and practicing everything there is to know about hitting (reading this book is a great start!). I highly recommend that players and coaches stay committed to the progression plan described earlier in this chapter because it sets a great foundation for how hitting should be taught and learned.

Teaching hitting is not an easy task, so coaches must put in just as much time and effort into learning as their players do. Players must stay consistent in their training during their off-season as well as during their regular season. This will not only impact their immediate on-field results but also their chances to compete at a higher level someday. The approach to batting practice should be geared toward each player's individual needs (on top of any team aspects), with the intent of challenging hitters to make improvements both mentally and physically rather than just taking hacks. When it comes to in-game hitting instruction, coaches and parents need to use extreme caution because the in-game approach should be mental, not mechanical.

Learning this information will give coaches a better idea of how to get the most out of their players. And players will learn how to get the most out of themselves!

End of the inning

Have fun. It's a game!

Chapter 8

9th Inning
Final Thoughts

The keys to achieving individual goals

Back in the day, when I was growing up playing baseball, there was no hitting instruction. There were no hitting coaches, no academies, no "select" teams with paid coaches, and definitely none of the technology and hitting tools we are blessed with today. Most of the time, our summer-team and high school coaches were just teachers or dads helping out. The only way we learned how to hit was by watching big-league games. You pretty much either figured it out yourself or you went and played something else. The harsh reality was that you could either hit or you couldn't. It was that simple.

Oh, how times have changed. These days it seems like everyone is a professional hitting instructor, and it's baffling for me to see how many kids today play baseball but hardly ever watch it.

I agree to some extent that you either have the physical and mental capabilities to hit or you don't. Quite honestly, there are certain things involved with hitting that you just cannot teach, and most great hitters naturally possess these important qualities. But in my opinion, "great" hitters make up maybe only the top 5% of all of the athletes who play baseball or softball. So what about the other 95% who aren't what we would think of as "studs"? Should they quit playing the game they love because they weren't born with the intangibles that a select few have? Absolutely not!

Athleticism, hand-eye coordination, and handling pressure and anxiety are all attributes that can be worked on and improved. I've seen many players dramatically enhance their hitting skills without having a lot of ability to start with. In fact, I've coached a couple of players who "overachieved" and were able to work their way into playing professional baseball. If you asked me if that were possible early in their careers, I probably would have said, *No way José.* These guys were by no means studs when they started, but they prove there is *always* a chance to maximize your potential if the work ethic is there.

Everyone has the potential, but not everyone has the work ethic to maximize it. If the potential is there, you must do whatever it takes to maximize whatever you have in you to be successful. You may not have the ideal mental and physical makeup to start with, but your hitting will improve with the right instruction and commitment. It does not matter if you naturally possess exceptional hitting talent. Your dedication, desire, and work ethic will dictate your ability to truly reach your full hitting potential and achieve your goals.

Caleb Hamilton

Whether that goal is to play at the highest level possible, to make your high school team, or to just have fun playing Little League, it doesn't matter. Working as hard as you can to become the best hitter you can be is the best way to help you accomplish your individual goals. The ultimate truth about baseball/softball is that if you can hit, you can play. In fact, I bet if I were to ask you who the best player is on your team, you wouldn't think of the best base runner, the best fielder, or the player with the strongest arm. You'd name the best hitter. All of these other skills are important, but there will always be more recognition and opportunities if you can hit. Any good coach in his right mind is not going to sit his best hitter for no reason. A coach will always find a way to get hitters in the lineup, even if it means throwing them out in left field and praying that no balls are hit their way.

Besides pitchers, how many Major League All Stars can you think of who can't hit? I can't think of one. There are obviously players who are known for their defensive skills, base-stealing ability, etc., but the best position players, at any level, earn recognition and prestige from their hitting. Of the five major tools a coach looks for in a player (hitting for average, hitting for power, arm strength, base running/speed, and defense), hitting will always be the most important. So baseball/softball players must make hitting the top priority in their skill development, because for players who love the game and have the desire to play for as long as they possibly can, their future depends on how well they can hit!

Bottom of the 9th

The brutal reality of hitting is that there are numerous fallacies and myths that have negatively influenced the way hitting is taught today. Because of this, a lot of coaches unknowingly hinder their ability to maximize the effectiveness of their hitting instruction. I highly encourage coaches and players to continue doing their own research in a relentless attempt to find what actually works for them and what doesn't, instead of yielding to popular misinterpreted hitting philosophies that don't work.

This book provides the most relevant information today about what you *really* need to know about hitting. It refutes and debunks misconceptions that do not give hitters the opportunity to maximize their success at the plate. In each chapter, I have thoroughly justified why certain things should or shouldn't be taught; to summarize them, here are my responses to 10 of the most common myths of hitting:

1.   There is no such thing as a perfect swing.
2.   Great swing mechanics alone don't make great hitters.
3.   The swing is neither rotational nor linear, it is a little of both!
4.   The front foot does not need to get down early, but on time.
5.   The "stay back" part of the swing happens after the body weight shifts.
6.   The bat path does not chop down on the ball.
7.   The barrel head is not above, or level with, the hands at contact.
8.   Hitters should never focus on an elbow slot, or lagging the bat.
9.   The hips and hands must work together at the same time.
10.   Extension is not a "pushing" motion, but a top hand whip.

There is a lot of information in this book. Players and coaches must be able to combine *all* of the elements of hitting and put them to use. It will take a vigorous effort to absorb it all, so be patient in the learning process but also be diligent in taking it all in. Focus on a few aspects at a time so there's no overload of information. You'll master specific elements of hitting quicker and make the learning process easier to comprehend.

Whether you're a player or a coach, one of the brutal truths about hitting is that success comes down to how badly you want it. Your dedication and perseverance will show how serious you really are about being the best you can be. Achieving excellence comes from desire. So I guess the question that every player and coach must answer is: Do you have the desire to achieve excellence?

Walking Off

There is no one to stop you but yourself!

Chapter 9

Extra Innings

H.I.T.: Honor, Integrity, Truth

What it means to be a H.I.T. Parent, Coach, or Player

Honor: *The courage to do what is right, no matter what. A belief that your actions represent more than just yourself; the recognition that what you do defines your entire generation.*

Integrity: *Doing the right thing even when nobody's looking.*

Truth: *1) The quality of being true, genuine, actual, or factual. 2) Something that is true as opposed to false. 3) A proven or verified principle or statement.*

As we near the end of the book, I'm asking for your help to raise the standards of accountability and sportsmanship within athletics.

I want to introduce you to H. I. T. , a commitment to honor, integrity, and truth in sports. It's a pledge to continuously motivate ourselves and others to be the best we can be, and to promote fun, competitiveness, discipline, focus, structure, and teamwork through athletics. Will you be a H. I. T. Parent, Coach, or Player?

How to be a H. I. T. Parent

As a H.I.T. Parent, you're raising a child, not an athlete. You pledge to:

- **Keep your perspective.** Celebrate the wins and individual accomplishments, but the value of sports comes from lessons about attitude, effort, preparation, and being a good teammate.
- **Relieve the pressure to perform.** You have no expectations beyond seeing your child give his best effort.
- **Add variety to life.** Faith, academics, family, friends, community activities, other sports—these are vital to a rich and varied life. Athletics shouldn't be your child's sole interest or passion, nor should it be yours.
- **Be a fan.** Sit in the bleachers where your kid can see you. Stay positive and enjoy all the players, not just your own. No swearing, no outbursts, no personal criticism. During the game, you're a fan, not a coach or an umpire.
- **Be consistent.** Treat your son or daughter the same regardless of the outcome of the game or the performance on the field.
- **Respect the coach.** He manages the games and runs the practices. If you have a question, talk to the coach face-to-face and never criticize the coach in front of your child.
- **Leave coaching for practice.** If your son or daughter wants to play catch, just go play.
- **Help your child manage time and gear.** Let him get his equipment together and dress himself. He should be responsible and accountable for being ready to go on time.
- **Share your experiences.** Help other parents when they ask about your experiences raising a child in sports.
- **Smile.** It's a game. It's supposed to be fun. If you're relaxed, your child will be relaxed. He'll probably have more fun and perform at his best.

How to be a H.I.T. Coach

Above all, a H.I.T. Coach is a positive role model for his players, parents, and those around him. You pledge to:

- **Make sports a positive experience.** Measure success not in terms of outcomes but in how each player improves as an athlete and grows as a young man or woman.
- **Be prepared.** Help your players be mentally, emotionally, and physically ready to give their best effort.
- **Be a role model.** Focus on what you can control, starting with your own attitude and behavior. No swearing, outbursts, or personal criticism. Be organized and learn your league's rules and bylaws. If you're having fun, your kids will be, too.
- **Be responsible to your players.** Whether you win or lose doesn't reflect your ability as a coach. Here's what does: your team's ability to demonstrate respect, humility, discipline, and a winning attitude.
- **Be there off the field.** Let your players know you're there for them off the field. Ask about school, family, and activities beyond sports.
- **Be vocal.** It's OK to be loud, but never with a hint of anger at the athlete personally.
- **Be responsible to your players' parents.** Communicate your expectations about games, practices, punctuality, and being equipped to play. Appreciate the parents' time, energy, and financial commitment involved with sports.
- **Smile.** A lot. It's contagious.

Be a H.I.T. Player: Tips to share with your team and son or daughter

A H.I.T. Player has fun, hustles, and puts his team before himself. H.I.T. Players pledge to:

- **Give 100%.** On the field and in the classroom. One without the other is not a winning combination.
- **Lead with your actions.** Let your work ethic be contagious. Treat others the way you would want to be treated, and respect your coaches, teammates, parents, opponents, and umpires.
- **Show good sportsmanship.** No bad language, and no making fun of your teammates or the opposing teammates.
- **Be emotionally fit.** No pouting, complaining, or talking back to coaches, umpires, or other players.
- **Be physically fit.** Take care of your body. Learn to train and eat right. No smoking, chewing, drinking, or drugs.
- **Thank your coach.** Shake his hand and say, "Thank you, Coach" after each game and practice. Help him by carrying the gear and keeping the dugout clear.
- **Keep your priorities straight.** Faith, family, school, friends—there are more important things in life than sports.
- **Be grateful.** Thank mom and dad for all they do for you.
- **Smile.** See a pattern here?

To Learn More

Never underestimate the power when we come together for a great cause. For more information, or to register to become a H.I.T. Coach or Parent, go to rijoathletics.com.

Extra Innings

Have Troy Come and Speak

I along with the professional staff at Rijo Athletics are available for clinics and camps for all facets of the game: hitting, infield, outfield, catching, pitching/velocity training, and coaching either at our facility or we can come to see you. We also give online evaluations and instruction for those individuals who can't travel to the Seattle area.

If your league, team, school, or academy would like more information about coaching clinics, lessons, or online instruction, or you have any further questions, please contact me at (425) 486-4878 or info@rijoathletics.com.

Follow Troy

Follow me on Facebook (TroyPSilva) and Twitter (TroyPSilva) to find out more about the *9 Innings of Hitting*. Leave your comments and learn what it takes to unlock your true potential as a hitter.

You can also learn more about me and Rijo Athletics at rijoathletics.com, and follow us on Facebook and Twitter (@RijoAthletics) for deals, specials, instructional tips, and more. You can also see free videos with drills and pointers on our RijoAthletics YouTube channel.

Thank you again for your time reading this book. God Bless!

—Troy

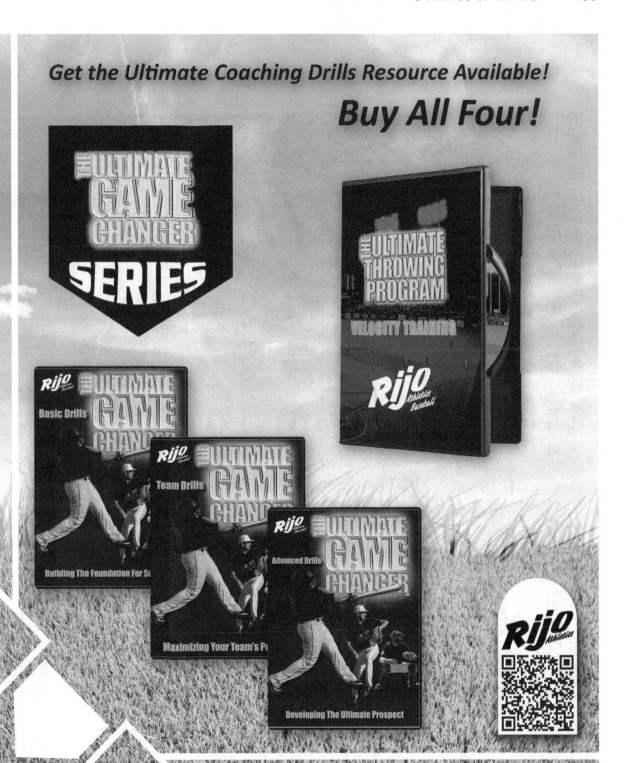

CPSIA information can be obtained
at www.ICGtesting.com
Printed in the USA
BVHW062320280619
552237BV00003B/30/P

9 781457 519574